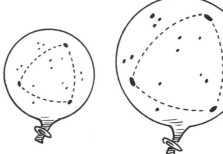

# Blue RIBBON

## *Science Projects*

STERLING

New York / London
www.sterlingpublishing.com/kids

Designed by Laura Hough Case
Illustrated by Glen Vecchione


STERLING and the distinctive Sterling logo are registered trademarks of
Sterling Publishing Co., Inc.

**Library of Congress Cataloging-in-Publication Data**
Vecchione, Glen.
  Blue ribbon science fair projects / Glen Vecchione.
    p. cm.
  Includes index.
  ISBN 1-4027-1073-9
  1. Science projects—Juvenile literature. 2. Science—Experiments—Juvenile literature.
I. Title.
Q182.3.V437 2005
507'.8—dc22

                                                    2005013557


10  9  8  7  6  5  4  3  2  1


Published by Sterling Publishing Co., Inc.
387 Park Avenue South, New York, NY 10016
© 2005 by Glen Vecchione
Distributed in Canada by Sterling Publishing
$^{c}$/o Canadian Manda Group, 165 Dufferin Street
Toronto, Ontario, Canada M6K 3H6
Distributed in the United Kingdom by GMC Distribution Services
Castle Place, 166 High Street, Lewes, East Sussex, England BN7 1XU
Distributed in Australia by Capricorn Link (Australia) Pty. Ltd.
P.O. Box 704, Windsor, NSW 2756, Australia


*Printed in China*
*All rights reserved*

Sterling ISBN-13: 978-1-4027-1073-5 (hardcover)
        ISBN-10: 1-4027-1073-9

Sterling ISBN-13: 978-1-4027-5067-0 (paperback)
        ISBN-10: 1-4027-5067-6

For information about custom editions, special sales, premium and
corporate purchases, please contact Sterling Special Sales
Department at 800-805-5489 or specialsales@sterlingpublishing.com.

# Contents

# Metric Equivalents

For many projects here you can round off metric equivalents for convenience. Be more careful if the project involves complicated math. Most measurements in this book, whether dry or liquid, assume capacity (liquid) measures in convenient milliliter conversions from teaspoons, tablespoons, and cups, etc. (Weights of these dry or liquid substances of course will vary.)

Accurate measurements and metric conversions are very important for sophisticated science endeavors: "The 'root cause' of the loss of the spacecraft was the failed translation of English units into metric units in a segment of ground-based, navigation-related mission software."—Arthur Stephenson, NASA chairman of the Mars Climate Orbiter Mission Failure Investigation Board, 1999

## Capacity (Liquid & Dry Measures)

1 milliliter = 0.2 teaspoon = 0.07 tablespoon = 0.034 fluid ounce = 0.004 cup

1 teaspoon = 100 drops = 5 milliliters = $\frac{1}{3}$ tablespoon

1 tablespoon = 3 teaspoons = $\frac{1}{2}$ fluid ounce = 15 milliliters

1 fluid ounce = 2 tablespoons = 30 milliliters = 0.03 liter

1 cup = 16 tablespoons = 8 fluid ounces = 240 milliliters = 0.24 liter

1 pint = 2 cups = 480 milliliters = 0.47 liter

1 quart = 4 cups = 2 pints = 32 fluid ounces = 960 milliliters = 0.95 liter = 57.75 cubic inches

1 liter = 1,000 milliliters = 61.02 cubic inches = 34 fluid ounces = 4.2 cups = 2.1 pints = 1.06 quart (liquid) = 0.908 quart (dry) = 0.26 gallon

1 gallon = 4 quarts = 128 fluid ounces = 3.8 liters = 231 cubic inches

## U.S. Dry Measure

1 pint = $\frac{1}{2}$ quart = 33.6 cubic inches = 0.55 liter

1 quart = 2 pints = 67.2 cubic inches = 1.01 liters

## Weight (Avoirdupois)

1 gram = 0.035 ounce = 1,000 milligrams = 0.002 pound

1 ounce = 28 grams = 437.5 grains = 0.06 pound

100 grams = $3\frac{1}{2}$ ounces

1 pound = 16 ounces = 454 grams = 0.45 kilogram = 7,000 grains

1 kilogram = 2.2 pounds = 1,000 grams

1 ton = 2,000 pounds = 0.9 metric ton

1 metric ton = 1,000 kilograms = 1.1 tons

## Distance

1 millimeter = 0.039 inch

1 inch = 25 millimeters = 2.54 centimeters = 0.025 meter

1 foot = 12 inches = 30 centimeters = 0.3 meter

1 yard = 3 feet = 36 inches = 90 centimeters = 0.9 meter

1 meter = 100 centimeters = 39.37 inches = 3.28 feet = 1.09 yards (1 yard + 3 $\frac{2}{5}$ inches)

1 kilometer = 1,000 meters = 0.6 mile

1 mile = 1,609.3 meters = 1.6 kilometers

## Area

1 square centimeter = 0.15 square inch

1 square inch = 6.45 square centimeters

1 square foot = 0.09 square meter

1 square yard = 0.83 square meter

1 square meter = 10.76 square feet = 1.19 square yards

1 acre = 160 square rods = 0.4 hectare = 4,047 square meters

1 hectare = 2.47 acres

1 square kilometer = 0.38 square mile

1 square mile = 2.58 square kilometers

## Volume

1 cubic centimeter = 1,000 cubic millimeters = 0.06 cubic inch

1 cubic inch = 16.38 cubic centimeters

1 cubic foot = 1,728 cubic inches = 0.028 cubic meter = 0.037 cubic yard

1 cubic yard = 27 cubic meter = 0.76 cubic meter

1 cubic meter = 1,000,000 cubic centimeters = 35.31 cubic feet = 1.3 cubic yards

## Temperature

To convert Centigrade (Celsius) to Fahrenheit degrees, use this formula:

$(°C \times \frac{9}{5}) + 32 = °F$

To convert Fahrenheit to Centigrade (Celsius) degrees, use this formula:

$(°F - 32) \times \frac{5}{9} = °C$

# Acknowledgments

*I would like to thank the following people for their assistance and support in writing this book.*

Jeanette Green, *editor extraordinaire*

Nancy Ahern
Sheila Barry
Lisa Blank
Randy Boyle
Eric Byron
Luca Cecchi
Peter Cicero
Jill Earick
Sabato Fiorello
Cliff Moon

Doug Reaney
Greg Sato
Ken Schlesinger
Gary Sosenko
Ted Strauss
Stephen Sturk
Bill Thomas
Josh and Irene Vecchione
Nick and Fran Vecchione
Nina Zottoli

Thanks to Mrs. Gillette's third grade class at
Brywood Elementary School, Irvine, California

Special thanks to Jim Ciccone for making it happen.

And as always, for Briana, Nicholas, and Isabella Vecchione

# Introduction

## Science Fair Season

It's science fair time of year again, time to begin to think about your project. Your parents, teachers, and friends all encourage you to do a good job—and you *know* you can—but it's finding a good, fresh idea that's the hardest part, and searching for the right project often keeps you from starting your project early enough to really enjoy doing it. After all, science fairs can be fun. Not only do they teach you about science, but you learn valuable organization skills in planning, information-gathering, project and time management, and teamwork. Entering a science competition can indeed be fun—and winning a prize is the most fun of all.

*Blue Ribbon Science Fair Projects* will get you started in the right direction. Each of the 100 projects here is designed to introduce new ideas, help you understand new concepts, and raise new questions in your mind. Each project will teach you, step by step, how to perform an experiment, demonstrate a procedure, or construct a working model that's guaranteed to get you "blue-ribbon" attention from the judges.

The projects have been organized to help you find the topic that most interests you. Although you'll find that some projects require model construction, other projects ask you to collect data and emphasize analyzing results. This means that we've included something for everyone—from constructing a levitating magnet to determining how rock music affects your workout; from building a plant model that demonstrates the Fibonacci series to determining what sort of cat food best suits your kitty. Other projects, like the "Gravity Well," even require a little game-playing activity by participants. It all adds up to fun, and having fun with science is a great way to learn about science.

## A Science Fair for Everyone

There are many varieties of science fair, some having particular themes that attract students interested in a particular field. For example, corporate-sponsored science fairs usually wish to promote new ideas applicable to the fields of telecommunications, robotics, computer science, biotechnology, or engineering. Awards in these types of competitions usually take the form of cash prizes. But other types of corporate-sponsored competition might offer the promising young scientist awards in the form of trips, scholarships, or even a chance to do some internship work in a prestigious lab.

The granddaddy of all science fair competitions is the Intel International Science and Engineering Fair (Intel ISEF). Started in 1947, the Intel ISEF is still the world's largest precollege celebration of science. Competitions, held annually in May, bring together over 1,200 students from 40 nations to compete for scholarships, tuition grants, internships, scientific field trips. In past years, the grand prize has been a $50,000 college scholarship and a high-performance computer.

Competitions—whether sponsored by corporations, universities, community groups, or a large organization like the Intel ISEF—are usually at the local or regional level, with finalists moving on to the regional, statewide, or even national level. This means that whatever your age, field of interest, or area of expertise—there's a science fair for you.

## Your Project and the Scientific Method

There's more to creating a good science-fair project than just coming up with a new idea and putting it all together. Science is all about observation, investigation, experimentation, and drawing conclusions. Creating a science-fair project should teach you something you never really knew before. And it should teach others—particularly the judges—something *they* never really knew before. It should do this in an original and engaging way. You must follow a logical procedure when you create a science fair project, and this

procedure is embodied in a system called the scientific method.

So what is the scientific method? Over the centuries, the scientific method has become the most important set of instructions for scientific discovery. As a logical system with its own set of checks and balances against human error, the method helps scientists make sure that their observations are accurate, their data reliable, their testing procedures carefully executed, and their conclusions well founded. More specifically, the scientific method researches a topic, asks a question, and then tests a potential solution, or *hypothesis*, by performing an experiment. The experiment, often repeated many times, yields data—the results—that either support or contradict the hypothesis. Following this procedure provides information, from which a conclusion is drawn, that will add to a general understanding of a topic.

Understanding the importance of the scientific method, each of the projects in this book is broken into steps that follow an abbreviated version of the method. Every project in *Blue Ribbon Science Fair Projects* has been organized into these sections.

- Materials (supplies for the experiment)
- Question
- Background
- Procedure
- Hypothesis
- Experiment to Test Hypothesis
- Results & Conclusions

Organizing the projects in this way allows you to see the scientific method in action. As you become more involved with your project, you are free to elaborate on any or all of these steps to suit your own curiosity, inventiveness, and ingenuity. And don't be afraid to depart from our instructions (while never ignoring the warnings!) and try something slightly different if that's where the project seems to lead you. You might find that a particular project idea could function as a springboard for something entirely new and original. Go for it!

## The Research Paper & Project Journal

Remember that your project consists of more than just building, mixing, or testing something. Most competitions require that you do some writing as well. This usually takes the form of both a research paper and project journal. The research paper goes into some depth about what is already known about the topic you chose for your project. It should also explain why the topic interested or challenged you. What do you think you can add to what is already known about this topic? Explain it carefully and clearly. Judges are always impressed by seriousness and professionalism.

At first, the research paper might seem like the most difficult part of doing a science fair project. But *Blue Ribbon Science Fair Projects* provides the seed of your paper in Step 3 of every project. Here we've provided enough information to get you going in the right direction— as long and as far as you'd like. But remember, this is only a beginning. The challenge is to make it yours.

As for keeping a journal, think of it as a scientific diary. Get yourself an inexpensive spiral-bound notebook and write about your project as you build and test it. Put your feelings into your journal. Science isn't just about doing, it's also about how you *feel* about what you're doing.

## How to Display Your Project

Even the most exciting project won't attract attention if it isn't displayed well. Taking the time to stage your project carefully and attractively can make all the difference in whether the judges spend a little more time than usual at your project or quickly move along to the next display.

All science fairs require that you display your project on a table and backboard. A backboard consists of a wooden, cardboard, or (more recently) foamboard stand that folds into three equal-size panels. The backboard should rest unsupported on the table and display prominently—in words, drawings, or photographs—all stages in the development of your project. The allowable size and shape of the backboard can differ among science fairs, so check with your teacher before you build or buy one.

Remember that the display doesn't have to be fancy. It's more important that you present your information clearly so that a judge can quickly understand what your project is all about and appreciate your efforts. "Tips from A Science Fair Judge" following this introduction will give you a better idea of what most science fair judges look for.

## So Who Are the Judges?

At all competition levels—local, regional, statewide, and even national—the judges come from three pools of professionals:

- Scientific professionals in the community, such as chemists, engineers, biologists, physicians, and psychologists
- Representatives from various corporations with an interest in a particular field of science, such as chemistry
- Teachers, writers, and researchers involved with science

Remember that judges look for creative and imaginative projects, the use of the scientific method, thoroughness in execution, skill in constructing the project, and clarity in the report writing. Rewards can range from cash, grants, or scholarship awards in each category (if the competition is ISEF-sponsored) or take the form of trips or internships if the sponsoring organization is a corporation, research institute, hospital, or any other organization with an interest in a particular topic.

## Supplies & Safety

*Blue Ribbon Science Fair Projects* are safe. When a project calls for the use of potentially hazardous materials, that project includes an "adult helper." Science is a serious business, and all project warnings should be taken seriously. Being cautious won't detract from your enjoyment of a project, but add to it. And care taken always means more accurate results.

Materials required to construct a project are inexpensive and easily found. Check hardware stores, art supply stores, hobby shops, and reliable online science supply houses, like Edmund Scientific. When appropriate, we suggest alternate materials for project variations.

## A Note About Measurements

Many project measurements include in parentheses equivalent metric measurements that can be rounded off for convenience. So, to simplify things, you could use 450 grams or even 500 grams in a project that calls for 1 pound of material, fully aware that the precise metric equivalent of 1 pound is 454 grams. Most measurements in the book, whether dry or liquid, assume capacity (liquid) measures in convenient milliliter conversions from teaspoons, tablespoon, or cups. Weights of these dry or liquid substances measured in teaspoons, cups, quarts, etc., will of course vary.

Since hardware and lumber are rarely found in American equivalents abroad, use the standard sizes found in hardware and lumber stores in your country.

To keep you going and ensure that finding equivalents is a quick and painless process, we include a Metric Equivalents table on page 219.

—*Glen Vecchione*

Here are helpful Internet sources.

www.odysseyofthemind.org
www.destinationimagination.org
www.intel.com/education/isef

# Tips from a Science Fair Judge

*Ted Strauss*

Some of the most fun I have is getting to judge the projects that students do for science fairs. Really! It's fun because I'm always amazed to see what students can accomplish and how creative they can be. At each competition, I do more than judge—I learn from your best efforts. I know that you are learning, too—not only about science but about making decisions, managing your time, solving problems, presenting what you have done, and working in a team (if it's a group project). These are all-important skills that prepare you for a life—in science or in any other discipline—and I get to see the result!

For the past 11 years, I've been a regional and state-level judge for many elementary through high school competitions. Two of them—Odyssey of the Mind and Destination Imagination—are more than science fairs because they present students with a variety of challenges, scientific or otherwise, that require a creative solution.

Participating in these organizations has helped me better understand just what I'm looking for when I see an award-quality project.

So, it's science fair time. You've worked hard for weeks. Naturally, your project is the best one because *you* did

it. But how do you let the judges know that? Remember that the judges are almost always following a scoring guide. We don't just look at a project and say, "It's good, but could be a bit better. I'll give it a score of 87." There are specific things we look for. Some of them are definite, such as "Is the hypothesis stated?" Others are more a matter of opinion, "Are the results described clearly?" As you do your project, keep in mind the elements that will be scored. It is always good if you include more, but be sure you have what is expected.

Personally, there are two things that bother me about some projects, and here is some advice on avoiding them.

First, be sure to collect enough data. Let's say your hypothesis is "Cats prefer to eat fish rather than chicken." Don't try with just one cat!

The second piece of advice is to change only one thing at a time. With the cat example, don't feed them fish in the morning and chicken at night. Now you have changed two things: what you feed them and the time you feed it to them. You cannot reach a valid conclusion by doing this. And don't be concerned if your hypothesis was wrong. Science is full of wrong guesses. That can be just as important as if you had been right.

Judges like to see an attractive display. The text should be readable. It doesn't have to be done on a computer; but if you write it out by hand, be sure to do it neatly. If you use a computer, don't use every font on your computer, or make each letter a different color. Special effects like those can be distracting and work against you.

Be very clear about what you are doing in your project. The scientific process is straightforward. What are you trying to do or show? What is your hypothesis about what the result will be? What steps did you follow? What equipment did you use? What data did you collect? Does the data prove or disprove your hypothesis? As judges, we want to see that you were truly "involved" with your project, that it wasn't just something you "had to do." And here's a hint: your project doesn't have to be complex. It's better to see a simple project done right than a complicated one that does not actually show anything.

When your display is finished, stop for a moment. Try to look at your display through the eyes of someone who doesn't know anything about your project.

Is it clear what you have done and what the results are? Is the display easy to read? Does it have the right amount of information? Imagine you are in a room full of projects, what makes yours *the one* that everyone wants to see?

If you have done a group project, make sure all members participate. Even if some in your group are not as "scientific" as others, *everyone* has something to contribute!

If part of the process is to make a presentation to the judges, be enthusiastic! Tell us what you did and what you learned. But also, tell us how much fun you had. Let us know what went well and what didn't. (Of course, stay within the time limit.) I know it can be scary to speak in front of us, but we are not there trying to find mistakes. We are truly interested in what you did. Remember, you are teaching us.

Give yourself plenty of time to do your project. It's human nature to delay. But you will have a lot more fun, and it will be much more interesting, if you give the project the time it deserves.

One of my regrets when judging is that there is a limited number of "winners." But believe me, if in doing your project you followed the process through to a conclusion, if you had to solve any difficulties, if you learned anything, or if it created some spark of curiosity in you, then you've come away with the biggest blue ribbon of them all—knowledge!

# One

# FUN *with Critters*

# Are Crossbred Dogs Healthier Than Purebred Dogs?

*Do crossbred dogs have fewer health problems than purebred dogs?*

## Materials
- 5-year medical records for 20 dogs (10 purebred and 10 crossbred) from a veterinary clinic or hospital. All dogs should be 5-year-old males.
- calculator
- posterboard (for chart)
- marker

## Background
People thinking about acquiring a dog may accept the notion that a purebred dog, or *pedigree*, will have more health problems than a crossbred dog. Dog adoption organizations make this claim to convince people looking for a dog to rescue a mongrel rather than to buy a pedigree from a pet store or breeder. A healthier dog means fewer visits to the vet and less expense. But does the evidence support the claim? This project seeks to find out.

To begin, let's clarify terminology. Although the terms are used interchangeably, a crossbreed is not the same as mongrel. A *crossbred* dog is produced when both parents are pedigree dogs but of different breed types. A *mongrel* dog is produced when either one or both parents are crossbreeds. The dogs used for this project were crossbreeds, not mongrels.

## Procedure
Five years of medical records for 10 male crossbred and 10 male purebred dogs are obtained through the cooperation of the local veterinary clinic or hospital. The records are examined for number and types of medical problems occurring over a five-year period. Comparisons between the two groups of dogs are made.

## Hypothesis
The records will reveal that, on average, the purebred male dogs have more health problems than crossbred male dogs.

## Experiment to Test Hypothesis
**1.** Ask your local veterinary clinic to provide five years of medical records for 20 male dogs—10 purebred and 10 crossbreed. The dogs should all be five years old.

# Veterinary Visits of Purebred 5-Year-Old Male Dogs 1999–2003

| Breed of Dog | Visits | Condition Type |
|---|---|---|
| Golden Retriever | 9 | dermatitis, ear infection, digestive problems, arthritis, hip dysplasia |
| Dalmatian | 11 | dermatitis, eye infection, digestive problems, hearing loss, bladder stones |
| Basset Hound | 12 | dermatitis, digestive problems, sores in mouth, bladder stones, eye infections, glaucoma |
| Dachshund | 10 | dermatitis, digestive problems, arthritis of spine, kidney problems, hypothyroidism |
| Great Dane | 8 | dermatitis, tooth decay/gum disease, fight injuries, arthritis, bladder stones |
| Irish Setter | 9 | dermatitis, eye infection, digestive problems, arthritis, hip dysplasia |
| Doberman | 11 | dermatitis, tooth decay, recurring cysts, arthritis, bladder stones |
| Pekingese | 7 | dermatitis, tooth decay, sores in mouth, arthritis, bladder stones |
| Rottweiler | 12 | dermatitis, gum disease, sprained shoulder, fight injuries, hip dysplasia |
| Chihuahua | 9 | dermatitis, eye infection, ear infection, fight injuries, arthritis |

# Veterinary Visits of Crossbred 5-Year-Old Male Dogs 1999–2003

| Mixed Breed | Visits | Condition Type |
|---|---|---|
| Labrador/Collie | 4 | dermatitis, ear infection, digestive problems |
| German Shepherd/Doberman | 3 | dermatitis, digestive problems, arthritis |
| Basset Hound/Terrier | 5 | dermatitis, digestive problems, cataracts |
| Sheltie/Beagle | 6 | dermatitis, digestive problems, urinary infection |
| Golden Retriever/Irish Setter | 4 | dermatitis, ear infection, tooth decay |
| Pekingese/Chihuahua | 4 | dermatitis, eye infection, digestive problems, arthritis |
| Terrier/Bulldog | 3 | eye infection, digestive problems, mouth sores |
| Boxer/English Setter | 4 | dermatitis, infected foot pad, urinary infection |
| Doberman/Rottweiler | 3 | dermatitis, ear infection, arthritis |
| Cocker Spaniel/Standard Poodle | 7 | dermatitis, digestive problems, eye infection, breathing difficulties |

**2.** Examine the records of the purebred dogs first, counting the total number of visits and determining which were the most common reasons for visits. Make a short list of the most common health problems affecting purebred dogs.

**3.** Examine the records of the crossbred dogs, following the same procedure.

**4.** Make a table containing your data and calculate the average number of visits per year for purebred and crossbred dogs.

## Results & Conclusions

The medical records supported our hypothesis. For purebred dogs, the total number of visits to the vet over a five-year period equaled 98. This was averaged to 19.6, or nearly four visits each year per dog. For crossbred dogs,

the total number of visits equaled 43, averaged to 8.6, or fewer than two visits each year per dog.

In addition, each of the purebred dogs showed genetically related health problems, such as hip dysplasia, glaucoma, and kidney problems. These were absent from the records of the crossbred dogs.

A final piece of possibly significant evidence was a fight injury entry in the records of the Great Dane, Rottweiler, and Chihuahua. Although two isolated entries prove little, it's commonly believed that pedigrees tend to have high-strung dispositions compared to crossbreeds.

For each mixed and crossbred dog, we discounted one visit to the vet for rabies and distemper shots. The rest of the data and results are summarized in the charts on page 15.

# Do Dogs Hear Music?

*Can a dog be trained to recognize two differently pitched notes as a single unit of sound?*

## Materials
- 2 puppies under 1 year old
- instrument, like a piano, guitar, or violin, capable of sounding discrete pitches
- knowledge of C major scale, or a musical friend to assist
- dog treats (salami is a favorite!)

## Background
It's long been known that dogs can hear nearly three times better than humans, particularly in the higher ranges. Whereas humans can hear within the frequency range of 20 to 20,000 Hz, the range for dogs is 15 to 50,000 Hz. Although you probably don't hear very much when you work on the computer, your dog (if he sits by you at homework time) is probably dazzled by a symphony of squeaks, hums, and whirrs coming from your hard drive.

Although dogs can hear and be taught to respond to basic sounds, the challenge in this project is to determine whether a dog can recognize a single sound event consisting of two separate notes played in sequence—in other words, a "melody." And beyond this, can a dog distinguish a sequence of two *identically* pitched notes from a sequence of two *differently* pitched notes?

## Procedure
Two 8-month-old female shelties, Betty and Scooby, are tested independently and the results compared. Each dog is given a treat after a sequence of two notes, the pitch C and G, is played on the piano. Neither is rewarded when a second sequence, consisting of two notes of the same pitch, is played. Training continues in 10-minute sessions daily for six weeks to see if either dog can distinguish between the same-pitched and differently pitched sequences.

## Hypothesis
Each dog will hear the two-note sequence as a single sound event. However, neither will be able to distinguish between the same-pitched and differently pitched sequences.

## Experiment to Test Hypothesis
*Described for one dog, Betty.*

**1.** Betty was held by an assistant and taught to sit quietly near the piano.

**2.** The player struck the note middle C on the piano, waited three seconds, then struck the note again. This sequence, with a 30-second pause between each set of notes, was continued for 5 minutes, after which Betty was allowed a break.

**3.** Resuming the session, the player struck the same two-note sequence of C's. But next, the player substituted the higher (by 5 scale steps) G note for the second C note on the piano. This time, Betty was rewarded with a treat. This C–G sequence was repeated for five minutes (with treats for Betty) before the session was concluded for the day.

**4.** The next day's session began with the C–G sequence followed by a treat. After 5 minutes of treats, Betty was allowed a break. Returning to the session, the C–C sequence resumed for 5 minutes with no treats.

**5.** The first half of the third day's session began with no treat, but treats were introduced 2½ minutes into the session and continued to the break. After the break, it was 2½ minutes of no treats followed by the 2½ minutes of treats.

**6.** The fourth day's session alternated no treats with treats—that is, the C–C sequence was played (no treat), followed 30 seconds later with the C–G sequence (treat). This 10-minute session, now finalized, was continued for another 60 days and Betty's behavior was observed.

## Results & Conclusions

Although variables in this project made conclusive results difficult to recognize, significant behavior was observed in both Betty and Scooby to partly disprove our hypothesis.

One factor complicated our results. Unlike Betty, Scooby was taught to recognize the C–G sequence first, which reversed the sequence of rewards/no rewards. But in all other respects, the procedures were the same and produced similar, surprising behavior in both dogs.

It appeared that, near the end of the two-month training period, both Betty and Scooby responded with more excitement after the differently pitched melody was played. But these results didn't appear until after about 40 days of training. Also, when the melodies were played on guitar and synthesizer neither dog recognized them.

At first, Betty appeared excited to just sit near the piano because she associated the piano "game" with treats. And, predictably, she looked to her trainer for a treat after only one piano note was played. But during the second week of training, Betty—while still excited at hearing only one note—became even more excited when the second note followed. This could be determined by seeing her wag her tail more vigorously than before. Betty seemed to understand that it was the two-note sequence that led to a treat, not the single, repeated-note.

Responding to the pitch difference was a more difficult behavior to recognize in Betty. But near the 40-day mark, Betty—while still wagging more vigorously after hearing the second note—seemed to completely break concentration and jump up at her trainer only when the second note played *was at a different pitch!* At this point she seemed confident that the two-pitch melody would inevitably lead to a reward, while the single-pitch melody was still a bit "iffy."

Since this behavior was mirrored exactly by Scooby in about the same time frame, it seems that both dogs developed a treat-driven appreciation for music.

# Does Your Dog See Yellow?

*Do dogs have color vision?*

## Materials
- female dog under 1 year old (She must know the command "Stay!")
- 3 sheets of paper in graduated shades of gray
- 3 sheets of paper in graduated shades of yellow
- camera with monochromatic film (or digital camera with color-removing software)
- 2 small opaque plastic food-storage containers (same size and sealable)
- marking pen
- dog treats (salami is a favorite!)

**Note:** *For more scientifically valid results, train three dogs simultaneously and triple the quantity of items on the list. Substitute blue and red for the other two female dogs.*

## Background
Scientists have long suspected that all breeds of dogs have some perception of color, but to what degree remains unknown. Today, sophisticated instruments allow scientists to study dog vision more accurately than ever before. Dogs have many more specialized vision cells, or *rods,* at the central portion of their retinas than do humans. Rods aid low-light vision and do not sense colors. But another type of cell, the *cone*, is more color sensitive.

Humans have thousands of cone cells; dogs have hundreds. On this basis alone, we can say that humans live in a much more colorful world than dogs. Still, just what a dog sees is worth investigating.

## Procedure
We attempt to train, independently of each other, three 8-month-old female Border collies to select a tinted paper over a gray one.

## Hypothesis
All three dogs will show some color recognition.

**Experiment to Test Hypothesis**
*This is described for one dog only.*

**1.** Make a row of three sheets of yellow paper, starting from the lightest yellow to the darkest. Underneath, make a row of three sheets of gray paper, from lightest to darkest.

**2.** Label the yellow sheets of paper Y1, Y2, Y3 to indicate their different shades. Label the gray paper G1, G2, G3.

**3.** Photograph (in black and white) each piece of yellow paper so that the label is clear. If using a digital camera, use the camera's software to remove color from the photos.

**4.** Print the photos and use the labels to pair up each shade of yellow (now gray) with its closest equivalent shade of true gray. Place these "matched" pairs of papers together and discard the extra paper.

**5.** Cut the papers into 2x2-inch (5x5-cm) squares, just large enough to fit over the covers of the food containers. Tape the yellow square to the cover of the first container, and tape the gray square to the cover of the second container. Put a treat in one of the containers and cover it with the yellow cover. Put the gray cover on the empty container. *Make sure both containers are tightly sealed.*

**7.** Choose a well-lighted, quiet place to begin your training session. Place the containers side by side. Separate them widely enough so that you can clearly see whether your dog chooses one container over the other.

**8.** Command the dog to "Stay!" about 6 feet (1.8 m) behind the containers, facing you. Then relieve the dog, allowing it to walk to the containers and investigate them. If your containers are sealed tightly, the dog will not show a preference. After two minutes, remove the cover of the yellow container and allow the dog to eat the treat.

**9.** Repeat this training every day for about six weeks using the yellow and gray containers. Each time, remove the cover of the yellow container after two minutes and allow the dog its treat. After about three weeks, alternate positions so that the yellow container is sometimes on the right, sometimes on the left.

**10.** Record the behavior of your dog throughout the entire training period. Count the number of times the dog "chooses" the yellow container over the gray container and compare this to the total number of tests for each session.

**12.** If your dog appears to be showing a preference, give it a final test by placing a gray square on both containers. Record the results.

## Results & Conclusions

The procedure described above was identical for the other two Border collies and the results were similar.

After four weeks of training, patterns began to emerge suggesting that each of the three dogs could identify color. In fact, our dog—trained with yellow—appeared to make color choices one week before the blue-trained dog and two weeks before the red-trained dog. This could be interpreted as evidence that dogs have more color sensitivity to primary yellows and blues and less for reds.

However, the results of this experiment might have been skewed by several conditions. For one, there's a potential difference in odor between a color-tinted paper and a monochromatic one. Each of the three dogs may have been making the "correct" color choice based on odor alone—a particular dog talent. Also, opening the treat container allowed odors to escape the container that could possibly have been absorbed in the square of colored paper. Again, the dogs may have chosen by nose alone.

Still, certain consistent behavior choices seemed to indicate that all dogs could identify color. This supports growing scientific evidence that dogs do indeed see colors, but not all colors. Humans, with our *trichromatic vision*, can detect all shades in the color spectrum. Dogs have *dichromatic vision*, which means that they probably see mostly in shades of yellow and blue and are less sensitive to greens and reds.

Many scientists now believe that although dogs have some form of color vision, color isn't particularly useful information to them, and so they tend to ignore it. Although herbivores might have the ability to see color in order to recognize ripe fruits and edible plants, for a terrestrial carnivore like the dog, it's probably more important to detect the shape of objects and to track motion, particularly in dim light.

# Birdsong at Dawn

*Do birds chirp more frequently at dawn than during any other part of the day?*

### Materials
- stopwatch or clock with second hand
- notepad and pencil

### Background
The sound of chirping birds can be a pleasant way to wake up on a spring morning, or it can be a noisy annoyance. If conditions are just right, a chorus of singing birds can easily transform from a pleasant twittering to a huge racket of screeches and squawks. Scientists suspect that morning temperature, light, and humidity all have something to do with it. The project will attempt to isolate the conditions that encourage birds to sing at their loudest.

### Procedure
For three days, the number of birdcalls will be counted at dawn for 3 minutes. Each call will be rated on a scale of 1 to 10 for loudness. The same procedure will be repeated at noon and in the early evening. Frequency and loudness of birdcalls will be compared among them three times of day.

### Hypothesis
A greater frequency of birdcalls will be recorded during the mornings and evenings than during the afternoons.

### Experiment to Test Hypothesis
**1.** Determine the hour of dawn for your region and season and set your alarm—this must be the same hour for all three of your morning observations.

**2.** Start the stopwatch (or watch the second hand on your clock) and begin counting birdcalls. Don't worry if you hear several calls at the same time. Record as many sounds as you can, and rate each for loudness on a scale of 1 to 10. Stop after 3 minutes and add up the number of sounds you recorded. Also make a note of any usual conditions like fog, rain, or unusually bright morning sunshine.

**3.** Repeat the above step at noon and at dusk. Make dawn, noon, and dusk observations for the next two days.

**4.** Compare your totals for each dawn, noting any differences. Compare totals for noon observations and dusk observations similarly.

**5.** Add the three days of dawns for total number of calls and degree of loudness. Do the same for the three noon and dusk measurements.

**6.** Compare totals for the three times of day and analyze results.

### Results & Conclusions

Birds were noisiest at dawn, followed by dusk. At noon, birdcalls were infrequent, although this may have been due to the presence of other sounds that made the calls more difficult to pick out.

Birdsongs averaged one song per two seconds at dawn, one song per seven seconds at dusk, and only two songs per minute at noon.

Dawn was consistently the wettest, quietest, and darkest time—all of which probably encouraged the best singing. At dawn there is little wind to rustle leaves and much less noise from people to compete with the birds' singing. And since physicists tell us that wet air transmits sound more effectively than dry air, moist dawn air means that birdsong can travel up to 20 times faster than in dry air. This means that a song may not actually be louder, it just carries farther. Finally, because light was low at dawn, singing is about all a bird could do. Low temperatures keep insect prey on the ground instead of in the air where they can be plucked and eaten. All of these conditions were most closely replicated at dusk and not at all at high noon.

# Measure the Protein in Commercial Cat Foods

*Does dry cat food contain more protein than canned cat food?*

## Materials
- 3-ounce (84-g) can "wet" cat food
- dry cat food
- calculator (or pencil and notepad)

## Background
Of all the meat eaters, the *felids* (cat family) have the most specialized diets. This is why biologists describe cats as *obligate carnivores*. The term means that a cat doesn't just prefer meat—it *requires* meat—and thrives with very little, if any, direct ingestion of plant material. But just as the herbivorous cow needs specialized digestive processes to convert grass to milk, the cat has also developed biochemical mechanisms to thrive on a diet rich in protein and fat, but lacking carbohydrates.

Cats need proportionally more protein in their diets compared with other mammals. An adult house cat requires about 30% protein in its diet compared to the 18% required for an adult dog. Cats require protein to maintain muscle, bone, ligaments, and tendons. Unlike dogs and humans, who can use carbohydrates in place of protein to supply energy, cats must *always* use a portion of their protein for energy. This is why a high-protein diet is important to a cat's health.

Many commercial brands of dry cat food claim that they contain more usable protein and less moisture than canned varieties and so offer the consumer better value for his or her money. In fact, when comparing the ingredients lists of dry and canned foods, the dry foods claim protein amounts of up to 40%—nearly four times the amounts listed on the canned foods. It seems reasonable. Canned food is a sloppy, smelly mess whereas dry food rolls out of the bag looking lean and clean and packed with protein. But is this really so? This project seeks to find out.

To calculate and compare the percentage of protein in dry and canned foods, each food "As Fed,"—that is, straight out of the bag or can—must first be converted into a standard volume of measurement called Dry-Matter Basis (DMB). The DMB shows the absolute amounts of proteins and nutrients in a food after all the moisture is removed. Most dry foods contain between 8% and 12% water and canned foods contain between 70% and 80% water. Converting AF (As Fed) to DMB is useful because it allows you to see the percentage of protein your commercial cat food actually contains under all that fancy gravy or crumbly stuff.

## Procedure

We measure and compare the protein content in two different kinds of cat food—wet and dry—using the AF to DMB formula. Results are compared with the manufacturers' percentage data and lists of ingredients for each product.

## Hypothesis

We will believe (at least for the time being) the manufacturers' claim that dry food contains proportionately more protein than wet food and represents a better value for the consumer.

## Experiment to Test Hypothesis

**1.** To convert AF into DMB for canned food, look at the ingredients list on the can to see what percentage of the food is moisture and what percentage is protein. For example, say you have a 3-ounce (84-g) can containing 78% moisture, 10% protein, and 12% other ingredients. This means that 22% of the can is dry matter made up of protein and other ingredients.

**2.** Divide 10% (percentage of protein) by 22% (total dry matter) for a quotient of 0.4545.

**3.** Multiply this quotient by 100 to get 45%. This is the DMB for our hypothetical can of food, and it shows that—minus the moisture—45% of what remains in the can is pure protein.

**4.** To translate into a volume equivalent, divide 22% in half to get 11%. This means that about 11% of a 3-ounce can of food is pure protein, and an adult cat would require two or three cans to get its minimal daily protein requirement.

**5.** Follow the same procedure for dry food. First determine the moisture-versus-protein content by reading the ingredients list on the bag. Let's say 3 ounces contains 10% moisture, 32% protein, and 58% other ingredients. This means that 90% of the food is dry matter made up of protein and other ingredients.

**6.** Divide 32% (percentage of protein) by 90% (total dry matter) for a quotient of 0.355.

**7.** Multiply this quotient by 100 to get 35%. This is the DMB for 3 ounces of dry food, showing what percentage is protein.

**8.** To translate this into volume you would calculate 35% of 90% to get roughly 31%. This means that 31%— roughly one third—of a 3-ounce quantity of dry food is protein.

## Results & Conclusions

The manufacturers are correct in claiming that dry food contains proportionately more protein than canned food. This means that although a quantity of dry food might be more expensive, it lasts longer than the equivalent amount of canned food and costs less per meal. The label on the brand of canned food we tested claimed 11% for protein, 14% for fat and fibers, and 75% for moisture. Our AF to DMB conversion supported this claim (with a margin of error of 2%). The label on the brand of dry food tested—a "premium" brand—claimed 40% for protein, 52% for "other ingredients" (unspecified), and 8% for moisture. Again, the AF to DMB conversion supported this claim, although we'd like to know more about those "other ingredients" listed!

# Wet Food or Dry—Which Do Cats Prefer?

*Do cats prefer wet or dry food?*

## Materials
- adult cat
- 6 ounces (168-g) dry cat food (Friskies Chef's Blend)
- 6 ounces (168-g) canned cat food (Friskies Turkey and Giblets)
- 2 small cat bowls, same size and color
- water
- measuring cup
- glass baking dish
- oven
- adult helper

## Background

A cat is not a sophisticated creature when it comes to its sense of taste. Whereas a human has close to 10,000 taste buds, a cat has fewer than 500. But like humans, cats can taste four basic flavors: sour, bitter, salty, and sweet. Cats are least sensitive to sweet, which is why you won't usually tempt your kitty with a Reese's Peanut Butter Cup.

Cats make up for their under-developed sense of taste by having a superb sense of smell. Estimates vary between breeds, but in general, cats have about 50 times as many odor sensitive cells as humans. Much of our experience of food flavor actually comes from how the food smells—but as humans, we know where to draw the line.

Take freshly ground coffee. For humans, something that smells so good is an invitation to taste it. But since the resulting taste is bad (when not brewed in water), we learn that—for ground coffee, at least—the "pleasantness" of the smell is a poor indicator of palatability. Similarly, something that smells "bad" (like cheese) doesn't discourage us from popping a sample in the mouth. Since the resulting taste is good (as it often is with cheese), we learn that—for cheese at least—the "unpleasantness" of the smell is *also* a poor indicator of palatability. In other words, the "intelligence" of a human's palate derives more from taste than smell, although the human nose will often color, ripen, and complicate our appreciation of food.

This is not the case for cats. Although a cat will use a similar blending of smell and taste to determine the overall palatability of food, the decisive factor for cats is how something smells. If you smear a piece of cat waste with enough fish oil, the cat will happily eat it and think nothing less of itself. For cats, the nose rules.

Other factors can affect a cat's appetite, too. Cats have the reputation of being "finicky" eaters, but this usually has more to do the texture or temperature of a food rather than how it tastes to them. Cats seem to prefer food that resembles the prey they would catch if they were in the wild.

In light of this information, our project seeks to discover whether wet or dry food is the preferred food of a cat—and whether, as cat owners, we should allow this preference to override the nutritional edge one food may have over the other.

## Procedure

We change our cat's diet so that he or she expects only a certain type of food at dinnertime. We then place a wet and dry version of that food before the cat and observe which is preferred. The experiment is repeated until a pattern of preference emerges from the cat's behavior.

## Hypothesis

The cat will display a slight preference for the wet food over the dry.

## Experiment & Demonstration

**1.** If your cat freely feeds on dry food but expects canned food at dinnertime, you must gradually change the cat's diet so it no longer freely feeds, and offer only one type of food at dinnertime. This will accustom your cat to expect food only at dinnertime and make test results easier to measure.

**2.** Prepare your cat for the test by alternating the two bowls at dinnertime. Allow your cat to feel comfortable feeding from either bowl.

**3.** If your cat is accustomed to dry food, divide 6 ounces of dry food between the two bowls and a cup of warm water to one bowl. Allow the watery bowl to cool to room temperature, then place both bowls in front of the cat. Observe which food—wet or dry—the cat chooses.

**4.** If your cat is accustomed to canned food, divide 6 ounces of canned food between one bowl and a heatproof dish. Place the dish, with an adult's help, in a warmed oven. Allow the food to bake (not burn!) until it's dehydrated, then remove it from the oven and let it cool to room temperature. Scoop the dried food into the second bowl and place both bowls in front of the cat. Observe which food the cat chooses.

**5.** Depending on whether you use dry or canned food, repeat Step 3 or 4 for a week, and keep track of how many times your cat chooses one bowl over the other. Add up the choices to determine if your cat is showing a preference for wet or dry food.

## Results & Conclusions

Any test of animal behavior should be performed many times and, preferably, with several animals so that behavior patterns can be averaged and generalized. Our observations were based on the behavior of only two cats—Brontë and Shrek. Still, the results were consistent and may very well indicate more generalized cat behaviors.

Without a doubt, both cats preferred the wet food to the dry. Even Brontë, who was raised on dry food, preferred water-moistened nuggets over the familiar dry ones. Shrek turned up his nose at the drier, baked version of his turkey giblet stew, and preferred the original wet stuff—straight from the can.

One thing was immediately apparent when preparing the bowls of wet food—wet food has a much stronger smell than dry food. Since a cat depends almost exclusively on its sense of smell to determine how good something might taste, it came as no surprise that the smellier food was the more appealing.

Another factor may have affected the food choice: water. Cats obtain most of their water from the moisture in foods. Water is important to a cat—especially an older cat—because an increased volume of water can prevent urinary tract problems by reducing the concentration of harmful minerals that sometimes accumulate in urine. As mature cats, perhaps both Brontë and Shrek sensed the need for increased water and so sought it in the wet food placed before them.

One factor that was not explored but might make for an interesting future project was the effect food temperature has on a cat's appetite. Since cats are such excellent sniffers, the steam-carried aromas of warmer foods would probably appeal. But does "warmer" mean "warm" or just warm enough to simulate the body temperature of freshly killed prey? Further research is needed.

# The Unhappy Carnival Goldfish

*Is a goldfish healthier living among water plants or in clear water?*

## Materials
- 2 small fishbowls (same size)
- 2 goldfish (same size)
- aquarium gravel
- water plants, like elodea, hornwort, or filamentous green algae (available in pet stores)
- water
- large bowl
- measuring cup

## Background
Have you ever seen a goldfish, alone in a bare bowl, waiting for someone to win it in a carnival Skee-Ball contest? You might wonder how long that poor fish can survive in its bare surroundings. Biologists know that all animals require certain essentials in their environment, such as comfortable temperature, breathable air, and nutritious food. It appears that the poor carnival goldfish lacks all three of these—or does it?

## Procedure
Each of two fishbowls (the same size) contains a goldfish. Plants, such as hornwort or algae, are added to one fishbowl only. The behaviors of the two goldfish are compared over the course of two days.

## Hypothesis
Since goldfish are not particularly intelligent animals and do not display emotions, no differences in behavior will be observed, even though one goldfish might be "happier" in its green environment than the other.

## Experiment to Test Hypothesis
**1.** Fill the large bowl with tepid tap water and allow the water to stand overnight. This allows minerals that might be harmful to the fish to either evaporate or settle to the bottom.

**2.** Use the measuring cup to scoop water from the large bowl into the two fishbowls. Add some gravel, and place a goldfish in each bowl.

**3.** Add a few water plants to bowl #1. Leave plain water in bowl #2.

**4.** Place both bowls in a bright spot, but out of direct sunlight.

**5.** Over the course of two days, observe and compare the behavior of the goldfish in the bowls. Try to make your observations at the same times each day.

**6.** After two days of observation, put both goldfish in a larger aquarium or donate them to a pet store.

## Results & Conclusions

Both goldfish displayed the same behavior during the first hour in their respective fishbowls. Each swam around the perimeter of the bowl, exploring. Checking back an hour later, it seemed that the goldfish in bowl #1 had found a "shady" spot among the plants and gently drummed its gills there, while the goldfish in bowl #2 continued to circle aimlessly. By evening, bowl #1 goldfish could be seen nibbling on the leaves of the water plants while bowl #2 goldfish still circled.

By morning, a marked change in behavior was apparent in bowl #2 goldfish. While the "happier" fish in bowl #1 was now swimming and exploring, bowl #2 fish had settled at the bottom of the bowl with its head against the gravel and its tail raised slightly. The motion of its gills seemed very slow. This sluggishness continued throughout the day, indicating—contrary to the hypothesis—an almost depressed fish, until both goldfish were rescued and placed in a larger aquarium.

It was clear from this project that green plants provide a healthier environment for goldfish. Green plants produce food and oxygen—the lack of which appeared to slow down the movement of the fish in bowl #2. Without food and oxygen, this goldfish would've moved into a dormant state to conserve its energy. Without help, it would soon die from both suffocation and starvation. Not only do plants help fish, but the plants benefit also. Since the waste products from goldfish contain minerals and nitrates that are useful to the plants, an aquatic system containing both fish and plants is ecologically stable.

# Two

# ASK a Friend

# Aging & Lung Capacity

*Do age and gender affect lung capacity?*

## Materials

- 2-liter (68-fluid-ounce) plastic bottle
- measuring cup
- flexible straw
- large bowl
- water
- 14 test subjects equally divided between males and females (Subjects should range in age from preteens to people over 60, with each age-group represented by a male and a female tester.)

## Background

Scientists who study aging tell us that lung capacity decreases as we grow older. On average, both men and women lose 20 to 25 milliliters of lung capacity for each year over age 20. This is because lung tissue becomes less elastic and less absorbent. Both biology and environment play roles in this. However, aerobic exercise (running, walking, cycling) can prolong the good health of the lungs and allow us to breathe more easily into our senior years.

Normal adult lung capacity is 3 to 5 liters (3,000 to 5,000 milliliters) and is calculated as milliliters of air per kilogram (2.2 kg = 1 pound) of body weight. The equation for women is 50 to 60 milligrams of air for each kilogram of body weight (55 mlxkg), and for men the equation is 70 milliliters per kilogram of body weight (70 mlxkg). Obviously, larger lungs have a greater capacity, so lung power before an individual reaches maturity is compromised.

This project seeks to test these facts with a simple measurement of lung capacity by displacing water with exhaled air in a 2-liter container.

## Procedure

Each test subject blows through a piece of rubber tubing into a water-filled 2-liter bottle, displacing water with air. Lung capacity is determined by measuring the volume of air collected in the bottle.

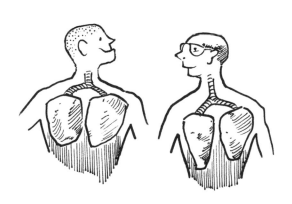

## Hypothesis
Lung capacity will decrease with age, as evidenced by the smaller volume of water displaced by the older subjects. In general, the males will show a greater lung capacity than the females.

## Experiment to Test Hypothesis
**1.** Plug the sink and fill it with water.

**2.** Fill the 2-liter bottle to the top with water. Place the palm of your hand against the mouth, turn the bottle upside down, and place it in the water so that the mouth is just beneath water level.

**3.** Push one end of the tubing through the mouth of the bottle underwater. Give the other end to your first test subject.

**4.** Have the subject take a deep breath and then blow through the tubing so that air will bubble into the bottle, pushing the water out. When the subject runs out of breath, remove the bottle and pour the remaining water into the measuring cup, noting the volume.

**5.** Repeat Steps 2 through 4 for each subject. Make sure you note the volume of water left in the water bottle.

**6.** To calculate lung capacity for each subject, deduct the remaining water from 2 liters.

**7.** Compare lung capacities among all test subjects and draw conclusions from the data.

**8.** Compare lung capacities between the males and females and compare data.

## Test Group

| Gender | Age | Gender | Age |
|--------|-----|--------|-----|
| M | 8 | F | 34 |
| F | 11 | M | 42 |
| M | 14 | F | 47 |
| F | 17 | M | 52 |
| M | 22 | F | 55 |
| F | 26 | M | 63 |
| M | 31 | F | 65 |

## Results & Conclusions
The chart above represents our test group. The subjects consisted of paired males/females representing preteens, teens, and 20- to 60-year-olds. The male and female participants in their 50s were both smokers.

The average lung capacity among all subjects was 0.56 liters. The average capacity for males was 0.62 and the average for females was 0.51. The greatest capacity was seen in the 22 to 34 age range, with peak capacities recorded for a 22-year-old male and a 31-year-old male.

Capacities for both males and females showed a noticeable decrease in the 40s. As expected, the youngest male and female showed a small lung capacity, but the lowest capacities were recorded for the male and female smokers in their 50s.

Although data (see the Results chart on page 36) clearly supported the hypothesis, the average capacity for all subjects fell well below the normal range of 3 to 5 liters for a mature adult. This

## Results of Age & Lung Capacity Experiment

| Age | Original Liters | Remaining Liters | Displaced Liters |
|---|---|---|---|
| 8—M | 2.0 | 1.7 | 0.3 |
| 11—F | 2.0 | 1.6 | 0.4 |
| 14—M | 2.0 | 1.5 | 0.5 |
| 17—F | 2.0 | 1.6 | 0.4 |
| 22—M | 2.0 | 1.0 | 1.0 |
| 26—F | 2.0 | 1.3 | 0.7 |
| 31—M | 2.0 | 1.0 | 1.0 |
| 34—F | 2.0 | 1.4 | 0.6 |
| 42—M | 2.0 | 1.3 | 0.7 |
| 47—F | 2.0 | 1.4 | 0.6 |
| 52—M* | 2.0 | 1.8 | 0.2 |
| 55—F* | 2.0 | 1.7 | 0.3 |
| 63—M | 2.0 | 1.4 | 0.6 |
| 65—F | 2.0 | 1.4 | 0.5 |

*indicates smoker

could be due in part to a flaw in the test design. Although the test was easy to set up, administer, and produced clearly measurable results, blowing through a narrow tube to displace water is a strenuous task that may have exhausted the subjects and skewed results. The poor performance of the smokers, when averaged into the other data, may have depressed results, also. Still, the general trends, as stated in the hypothesis, were supported.

One factor that was not explored was the relative fitness of each subject and how it could affect results. This could be the basis for a future study.

# Beverages & Tooth Decay

*Which beverages induce the most tooth decay?*

## Materials
- 4 dog or cat teeth
  (ask your veterinarian)
- 4 small jars with lids
- measuring cup
- measuring spoon
- bleach
- water
- milk
- orange juice
- cola
- pot (for boiling water)
- latex gloves
- old toothbrush
- paper towels
- adult helper

## Background
Millions of people throughout the world suffer from tooth decay. The health of our teeth can be an important factor in the overall health of our bodies, and cavity prevention is one of the most basic goals of good personal hygiene. But it's not always easy to tell which foods or beverages are the most harmful to teeth. This project seeks to examine the effect of four common liquids on tooth enamel.

## Procedure
Each of four teeth is soaked in water, milk, orange juice, and cola. The teeth are kept in labeled jars, have their fluids replaced weekly, and refrigerated for three weeks or until noticeable decay is present.

## Hypothesis
Acidic beverages like orange juice will be the most destructive to tooth enamel.

## Experiment to Test Hypothesis
**1.** Clean the teeth by soaking them for 2 minutes (no longer!) in 1 cup of water mixed with 1 teaspoon of bleach.

**2.** Put on the latex gloves. Remove the teeth and scrub each tooth with an old toothbrush. The teeth should be uniformly white and free of stains.

**3.** Have an adult help you boil the glass jars and lids. Boiling sterilizes the jars so that harmful microbes won't grow on your samples and spoil the results. Allow the jars to dry and cool before continuing.

**4.** Place a tooth in each jar. Label one lid WATER (the control), the next MILK, the third ORANGE JUICE, and the fourth COLA. Place the lids on the jars.

**5.** Fill each container with 30 milliliters (about 1 fluid ounce) of each liquid and place the appropriate lid on each jar.

**6.** Store the jars in the refrigerator—down on a bottom shelf where they won't gross anyone out!

**7.** Allow the teeth to remain refrigerated one week and record any changes you see. After a week, replace the liquid in each jar. Allow the teeth to remain for up to three weeks, replacing the liquid in the jars each week.

**8.** The experiment is over when one of the teeth shows noticeable signs of decay. At this point you can remove all teeth, rinse them in soapy water, and compare results.

## Results & Conclusions

As expected, the water-soaked tooth showed no decay at all. Nor was there any discoloration apparent on the tooth enamel. The milk-soaked tooth showed one small cavity on the tooth's side in addition to various white splotches that appeared to be calcium deposits which could not be rubbed off. The tooth soaked in orange juice showed extreme discoloration—yellow and brown patches all over the enamel—but only two small cavities located near the tip of the tooth.

Contrary to the hypothesis stating that the acidic orange juice would cause the most damage, the tooth soaked in cola showed five cavities as well as a deep brown discoloration. Two of the cavities were big enough to compromise the strength of the tooth, and it appeared that even the pressure of one normal bite would shatter it. Clearly, the cola contained the most sugar of the four liquids and had the most destructive effect on tooth enamel.

But how does sugar actually destroy teeth? Our research revealed that sugar, particularly sucrose, contains sticky *glycoproteins* (a combined carbohydrate and protein molecule) that stick to the teeth to form the filmy bacteria called plaque. At the same time, another type of bacteria, *Streptococcus mutans*, grows on top of the glycoprotein. This plaque-loving streptococcus creates a new substance—lactic acid—which dissolves the calcium phosphate that tooth enamel is made from. The result? A cavity.

# Does Chewing Gum Improve Memory?

*Does chewing gum improve recall in a word-sequence memory test?*

## Materials
- 6 friends as test subjects (3 males and 3 females)
- stick of chewing gum for each subject
- pen and paper for each subject
- 2 lists of 20 words (same words, different order)

## Background
This project will attempt to measure whether short-term memory is enhanced by chewing a piece of gum. Scientists have long suspected that mental functioning can be improved by muscle activity. In the nineteenth century, this was first observed in the behavior of mathematically gifted individuals who, to perform at their best, all expressed a desire to walk briskly around the room while doing mental calculations. Many creative people will tell you that they get their best ideas, or solve problems most effectively, while doing some form of light exercise, such as walking. But only in the past decade has the relationship between muscle activity and memory been seriously explored.

Recently, Japanese researchers found that activity in the hippocampus, an area of the brain important for memory, increases while people chew. Further research suggests that insulin receptors in the brain may be involved too, since chewing releases insulin because the body is expecting food. But opinions differ among scientists. It could be that chewing gum simply increases the heart rate, thus improving the delivery of oxygen to the brain and enhancing its cognitive powers.

## Procedure
Subjects—first without chewing gum—are read a list of 20 words and write down the list as they remember it. Subjects are then given a piece of gum and read a second list consisting of the same 20 words but in a different order. Test results are compared.

## Hypothesis

The subjects will perform better while chewing gum.

## Experiment to Test Hypothesis

**1.** Choose object words (nouns), such as *house*, *tree*, or *book* for your word lists.

**2.** Give each subject a pen and paper.

**3.** The tester reads the first list of words at the rate of one word per second. The tester says, "List finished," after the last word.

**4.** Subjects write down the sequence of words as accurately as they can.

**5.** Each subject receives a piece of chewing gum and is allowed to chew for about 1 minute.

**6.** The tester reads the second list of words, again at the rate of one word per second. The tester says, "List finished," after the last word.

**7.** Subjects write down the second sequence of words and test results are compared.

## Results & Conclusions

Since aging can affect memory, it was important to recruit subjects who were all about the same age—in this case, all 14 year olds. Three were females and three were males. Also, since the ability to recall a word is influenced by the word's position on the list (first and last words being the easiest to remember) we factored in that the top and bottom words would be the most accurately remembered.

Still, overall word recall of the second list was much better than the first list, and (as expected) this was much more apparent for words in the middle of the list. After the first list was read, three of the six subjects recalled 5 words in the correct sequence, or only 25% of the total words. Two recalled 6 words (30%), and one recalled only 4 words (20%).

After the second list was read with the subjects chewing gum, 5 of the subjects recalled 8 words (40%) and one recalled 7 words (35%). Although this wasn't formally measured, it also seemed to take subjects less time to write down their recollected lists.

# Does Music Affect Dinner Conversation?

*Does the type of music played affect how much we eat, the time it takes us to eat, and how much we talk over dinner?*

## Materials
- CDs of classical music
- CDs of popular music
- one family, gathering for various lunches or dinners
- hidden tape recorder
- clock or timer

**Note:** *Let one adult family member know that this is a science project and urge him or her to cooperate with you if someone should object to your choice of music during the meal(s).*

## Background
Music has long been known to induce different emotions and psychological states in people. While some music is composed to excite people, other music encourages relaxation or even conversation. People who manage restaurants devote much time and attention to the type of music—if any— played for customers. Data have shown that, when it comes to eating out, the right choice of music can encourage diners to stay, eat more, talk more, and even leave a better tip. Although this project tests these ideas in a very limited manner, significant results can be obtained with careful planning and observation.

## Procedure
Interaction among the same eight people at the dinner table is observed and recorded on three occasions. (For this project, the dinners were all outdoor barbeques.) The first dinner has no background music. The second dinner is accompanied by classical music (Mozart). The third dinner features a selection of pop tunes performed by the groups Creed and Vertical Horizon.

## Hypothesis
Dinner will take longer and there will be more conversation without music. Classical music will make for a shorter dinner, and pop music will result in the shortest of the three dinners.

## Experiment to Test Hypothesis
**1.** Make sure you start with a group of people already acquainted and remain with that group for each of your testing dinners. Our group was made up of the tester (Briana, 12 years old) and her best friend. Briana's mother, father, brother (7 years old), grandmother, grandfather, and uncle were all present, too.

**2.** Note the time and quietly switch on the tape recorder when everyone sits down to eat. Observe what is talked about, how much people eat, and whether laughing or arguing occurs. Record the time dinner ends (everyone leaves the table and plate clearing begins) and stop your recording. Label the tape "No Music."

**3.** Repeat this procedure for the next dinner, but this time play the classical music CD in the background. Make sure the music is at a volume level suitable for conversation. When dinner is finished, label the tape "Classical."

**4.** For the third dinner, play the pop music CD, observing and labeling as before.

**5.** Compare your notes for all three dinners. Then compare the tape recordings you made, listening for laughs, arguments, subjects of conversation, and who's doing the most talking. Also pay attention to the general noise of people eating. What can you say about how music might have affected each of the dinners?

**Results & Conclusions**

Several variables made definitive results for this project difficult to recognize. Different food was served at each barbeque—burgers the first time, steak the next time, and chicken the third time. Briana's dad likes steak more than chicken and so was probably in a better mood for that meal than for the others. But since other eaters, like Briana's friend, enjoyed chicken more than steak, it was hoped that this food variable would be minimized.

Significant overall patterns were recognized between the three meals. Contrary to the hypothesis, the dinner without music was basically shorter and had less conversation than the dinners with music. There were long pauses between short conversational exchanges with lots of eating noises on the tape recording. Most conversation took the form of short questions from adults and shorter answers from children. Adults did less talking to one another. Also, there seemed to be much more commenting by adults on what was being eaten by the children, as if the dietary habits of the children were being scrutinized.

The classical music dinner featuring Mozart showed a surprising shift in the conversation. The adults talked more to each other and seemed to pay less attention to the children. Also, the conversation became less about food and more about other people and events of the day. Dinner with Mozart was both longer and shorter—longer, because the adults sat around the table and continued to converse in a more serious "adult" tone; shorter, because the children finished early and left the table.

But the dinner with pop music proved the most successful of all in terms of ongoing conversation, laughter, and true exchanges between children and adults. It seemed as if the music—first some mildly upbeat ballads from Creed and then a sampling of tunes from the group Vertical Horizon—relaxed everyone and put the focus on just having a good time. This was true for even the sadder songs. The music seemed to appeal to both adults and children since both left the dinner table at about the same time. Perhaps the presence of song lyrics (as compared to just orchestral music) made a difference by encouraging conversation, but it was clear that this was the happiest table of diners—one that would probably leave a good tip if they were in a restaurant!

# Gender & Sense of Smell

*Do boys and girls have an equally sharp sense of smell?*

---

## Materials
- 3 identical squeeze bottles with slide caps
- measuring spoon
- ⅛ teaspoon mashed banana
- ⅛ teaspoon chopped onion
- ⅛ teaspoon grated Parmesan cheese
- 10 friends (five boys and five girls) as test subjects

## Background
Scientists who study the brain have noted only slight differences in brain structure between males and females. So far, studies that have looked at differences in the brains of males and females have focused on three areas: total brain size, a part of the brain called the corpus callosum (the great band of fibers that connects the cerebral hemispheres), and another part called the hypothalamus.

Still, the debate goes on as to whether, behaviorally, a female may respond differently than a male in a given situation because of biology alone, environment alone, or a complicated interaction of the two. For example, females are supposedly better in certain language abilities and males are better in spatial abilities. For years, scientists have tried to find differences in the right and left cerebral hemispheres to support this idea. However, few of these experiments have found meaningful differences between the brains of males and females. In fact, there are many more similarities than differences between the cerebral hemispheres of both genders.

One thing is clear, however: Hormones present during a baby's development affect the brain and determine whether the brain will be female or male. A male brain is about 5% larger than a female brain but doesn't necessarily contain more brain cells. In fact, research shows that female brains have about the same number of cells packed into a smaller space. This packing may be responsible for a different network of connected cells in females—one that favors the right side of the brain to process sensory information over the left side of the brain. Such a difference may have advantages as well as disadvantages, as this project will attempt to demonstrate.

## Procedure
Three squeeze bottles with sliding caps contain respectively ⅛ teaspoon of mashed banana, ⅛ teaspoon of chopped onion, and ⅛ teaspoon of grated

Parmesan cheese. (One-eighth teaspoon = a "pinch" of a dry ingredient.) Five males and five females are exposed briefly to each odor, rate its intensity, and are asked to identify the substance.

## Hypothesis

A slight, but significant difference will be detected between the smelling skills of boys and girls.

## Experiment & Demonstration

**1.** Mash a banana in a plate and scoop ⅛ teaspoon of it into the first squeeze bottle. Screw the lid on the bottle and make sure the slide cap is tightly shut.

**2.** Repeat this procedure with the chopped onion and grated Parmesan cheese.

**3.** Use the tape and marker to make labels identifying each substance, small enough so that they can be hidden from your test subjects when you hold the bottles up for sniffing.

**4.** Open the slide cap on the bottle containing the banana mash and hold it up to the nose of the first male subject. Give the bottle a quick squeeze and then remove it from the subject's nose, asking him to identify the odor. With the same male subject, repeat this procedure using the bottles containing the chopped onion and grated cheese, each time asking the subject to identify the odor.

**5.** Repeat the previous step—this time with a female subject. However, for the next pair of male and female subjects, change the order of the bottles. Continue exposing subjects to the odors until all subjects have been tested.

**6.** Tabulate answers to determine which gender best identified the smells.

## Results & Conclusions

The girls of the test group could readily tell the stronger odors from the weaker ones. All reacted instantly and negatively when they smelled the cheese and onion. The boys, however, took longer before they recognized the "unpleasantness" of the cheese or onion smell and reacted to it. Both boys and girls took about the same time to react to the banana smell, which they described as "fruity."

When it came to identifying the particular substance, however, it appeared that the girls had only a slight advantage over the boys. Only one of the boys mistook the cheese for "garlic" whereas all of the girls correctly identified it. So the difference in gender was reflected more in the intensity of the smells rather than in their identities.

Although the results of this test might point to tantalizing differences in the way males and females perceive odors, certain variants must be taken into account before a firm conclusion should be reached. For one thing, girls may be conditioned to react more quickly to bad smells due to their sensory familiarity with more pleasant odors—foods, sweet-smelling flowers, perfumes, and the like. Boys might much more readily identify odors such as smokes, woods, metals, and industrial products such as waxes. In other words, sensitivity to odor might be more a factor of training and environment than because of any difference in brain structure. More investigation is needed.

# Handedness & the Brain

*Does a right-handed person also show a preference for using the right foot, eye, and ear? Is the same true for a left-handed person?*

## Materials

*For testing right-handedness and left-handedness*
- pencil
- note paper
- scissors
- ball
- fork
- drinking glass

*For testing right-foot and left-foot lateralization*
- large ball (for kicking)
- stepstool

*For testing right-eye and left-eye lateralization*
- cardboard tube
- medallion on a chain

*For testing right-ear and left-ear lateralization*
- tuning fork
- small, rattling box
- 30 friends as test subjects

## Background

The human brain is a paired organ composed of two halves, called cerebral hemispheres, which look almost exactly alike. But despite their anatomical similarities, the two halves of the brain function differently. Scientists coined the term *brain lateralization* to point out how each half of the brain is responsible for a unique set of tasks.

In the mid-1800s, Paul Broca, a French neurosurgeon, identified an area in the left hemisphere that plays an important role in speech production and language comprehension. However, the emotive content of speech appeared to be located somewhere in the right hemisphere. To this day, scientists are still trying to map exactly what each brain hemisphere does and whether a person can be characterized as a "left-brain" or a "right-brain" thinker.

This is where the concept of "handedness" comes in. Most people define handedness as the hand you use for writing. But researchers have broadened the idea by including the hand that performs faster or more precisely on manual tests, or the hand that you just prefer to use, regardless of performance. Also, handedness has been expanded to include a general preference (motor and sensory) for one side of the body over the other—a phenomenon this project will try to demonstrate. Finally, recent research has shown that handedness is not absolute but comes in varying degrees. A person can be right (or left) hand exclusive, preferential, or show no preference for either hand (ambidextrous).

Handedness is important to researchers because Broca suggested that it could show which brain hemisphere was the more active in a person and provide important clues into someone's verbal, emotive, and reasoning abilities. Broca also suggested that hand preference indicated the *opposite* hemisphere preference. In other words, left-handed people were right-brained and right-handed people were left-brained.

## Procedure

Each subject is tested for right-handedness or left-handedness and placed in a group reflecting the degree of preference. The subjects in each group are then tested to see if they also prefer their right foot, right eye, and right ear. Correlations between handedness and a more general body orientation are made for each of the groups.

## Hypothesis

A right-handed person will clearly prefer his right foot, right eye, and right ear. A left-handed person will display a similar left foot, eye, and ear preference.

## Experiment & Demonstration

**1.** Each subject was first tested for right-handedness or left-handedness. This was accomplished by having each subject write his name, cut out a circle with a pair of scissors, throw a ball, pick up a fork, and drink from a glass.

**2.** Depending on how a subject performed on the above series of tests, he or she was placed in one of five groups—(1) right-hand exclusive, (2) right-hand preferred, (3) ambidextrous, (4) left-hand preferred, and (5) left-hand exclusive.

**3.** Each of the five groups was put through the following two tests for foot-preference: kicking a ball, and mounting a step stool (to observe which foot leads).

**4.** Each of the five groups was put through the following two tests for eye preference: looking through a cardboard tube (to observe which eye was used to peer through the tube), and swinging a medal in front of both eyes to see which eye was quicker to follow the motion.

**5.** Each of the five groups was put through the following two tests for ear preference: head turn direction choice to better hear a tuning fork placed directly in front of the face, and observing which ear the subject chose when asked to listen to the rattle inside a box.

**6.** The tests were repeated three times, and the degree of overall left or right orientation was determined for each subject in a group.

## Results & Conclusions

The biggest group (17 subjects) was the right-hand exclusives, followed by the right-hand preferred group (9 subjects). One participant seemed truly ambidextrous, two seemed left-hand preferred, and only one was left-hand exclusive.

In the right-hand exclusive group, all of the subjects preferred their right feet, and all but one subject also preferred right eye and right ear. In the right-hand preferred group, five of the nine subjects chose their right feet, eye, and ear. The remaining four had no preference.

The ambidextrous subject could perform all tasks equally well with either hand, eye, or ear.

Among the two members of the left-hand preferred group, one subject chose the right foot to the left foot, and the other chose the left foot but the right eye and ear. However, the biggest surprise (which contradicted the hypothesis) came with the single left-hand exclusive subject. Despite her exclusive left-handedness, this subject chose her right foot, right eye, and right hand for all the subsequent tests. These results seemed to suggest that although right-hand exclusiveness is generally followed by a total right-body orientation, this is not the case for left-hand exclusiveness. The conclusion isn't airtight, however, and to improve accuracy, the tests should be repeated with another left-hand exclusive subject.

# Music & Exercise

*Does the type of music played in a gym affect how long people exercise?*

## Materials
- 3 classical music CDs
- notebook for recording data

**Note:** *Arrange to have the desk people at your local gym assist you with this project by playing your music selection for one hour at a given time of day and then clocking the check-in and check-out times of customers during that hour.*

## Background
Music has long been known to induce different emotions and psychological states in people. Some types of music help people relax or think; other types inspire people to tap their feet or dance. Some music demands active listening, while other music fades into the background so that conversation is easier. Choosing the right kind of music for a social, business, or activity-oriented environment is important to its success. This project seeks to explore that relationship.

## Procedure
At a local gym, the usual pop music track is replaced with several classical music selections. This replacement occurs for three consecutive Wednesdays between 11 A.M. and 12 P.M. Customer attendance and workout behavior during "classical-music hour" is compared to "pop-music hour."

## Hypothesis
Customers will spend less time exercising when classical music is played.

## Experiment to Test Hypothesis
**1.** Gather attendance data at a local gym between the hours of 11 A.M. and 12 P.M. on three consecutive Wednesdays. This can be obtained by having the desk people tabulate the number of clients checking in or out during that time and calculating the length of an average workout.

**2.** Make a log of the type of music and song titles played during these times.

**3.** Choose three CDs of classical music. Each CD should contain about one hour of music. (Our selections included Bach, Tchaikovsky, and Beethoven—all orchestral works.)

**4.** For three consecutive Wednesdays between 11 A.M. and 12 P.M., replace the usual music with one of the classical music CDs. During those times, remain at the gym to observe workout behavior. Listen to conversations among clients and take notes.

**5.** After your six-week testing period, ask the desk people to help you average and compare attendance and workout duration data for regular and classical music Wednesdays. Compare that data with averaged data for regular Wednesdays.

## Results & Conclusions

Several factors contributed to the unexpected complexity of this project. First, it was important to determine the age and gender of the people using the gym on Wednesdays between 11 A.M. and 12 P.M. From the client database, it was shown that about 65% were young women between the ages of 25 and 33 (Group A). About 28% were young men of the same age range (Group B). The remaining 7% were equally divided between men and women over 45 (Group C). Second, it was important to identify the music played on a typical Wednesday to see if it was consistent in style, mood, and general energy level.

An analysis of client data for typical (nonclassical) Wednesdays revealed that an average of 32 customers checked in and 6 customers checked out between 11 A.M. and 12 P.M. The customers who checked in were mostly Group A. The customers who checked out were equally divided between Group A and Group C. The music played consisted entirely of hits from current pop artists—mostly high-energy, high-volume love songs.

In contrast, client data for the first classical Wednesday revealed that although 28 customers checked in between 11 A.M. and 12 P.M., 13 customers checked out during the same hour (while Bach's Orchestral Suite No. 2 was played). Similar results were observed for the remaining two classical Wednesdays.

The customers who checked out were mostly in Group B—the young men, with a few young women. Comments overheard among young men while exercising ranged from recognizing and disliking the type of music being played to simply feeling "tired" or "in a bad mood." Not surprisingly, the type of classical music played did little to alter this negative attitude during the classical Wednesdays. Bach and Beethoven were both generally disliked. Fast and slow movements of Tchaikovsky's *1812 Overture* did little to inspire people on their treadmills. This dislike was not shared among the Group C (over 45) clients. Interestingly, there was only one Group C checkout for the entire time classical music was played.

The results of this project show that the hypothesis was only partially correct. It's true that high-energy pop music, with lots of variety and mostly understandable lyrics, seems to inspire young men and women to exercise harder, longer, and generally ensures them a more pleasant workout environment. However, clients of both genders over the age of 45 appear not to be negatively affected by the classical music and may even be encouraged to relax and enjoy their exercise period more.

# Phantom Hands Illusion

*Can a dramatic retinal afterimage of hands be created using only a bright light and darkened room?*

## Materials
- dark room
- high-intensity shielded desk lamp
- black bath towel
- 3 friends as test subjects

## Background
The human eye is a complex organ because it must perceive and communicate a stream of complex visual information to the brain. But when it comes to "seeing," the brain does most of the work. It's the brain that corrects the upside-down image of your eyes so that you see the sky above and the ground below. It's the brain that recognizes faces and objects from a jumble of forms and colors. It's also the brain that decodes motion, shade, and color, allowing us to make sense of our surroundings.

But even without the brain, the eye is a sophisticated instrument, the workings of which can be examined. One of these workings will be examined in this project—how the eye processes light in the sensitive lining of the retina.

## Procedure
After sitting in the dark for two minutes, three subjects have their hands suddenly illuminated by a burst of bright light. Subjects remain in the dark for several minutes to experience the retinal afterimage of hands.

## Hypothesis
A bright, three-dimensional phantom image of hands will appear before each subject's eyes.

**Experiment to Test Hypothesis**

**1.** Place the towel on the floor and position the lamp over it, facing down. Make sure the lamp is shielded so that it throws light downward only.

**2.** Subjects sit in a tight circle on the floor surrounding the lamp. Each of the three subjects places one hand in the center of the circle so that the hands pile up. The tester positions the lamp directly over the hands without blocking any subject's view of the hands.

**3.** When everyone is sitting comfortably, the tester gets up and switches off the room light. He instructs everyone to sit quietly and keep their hands very still. The silent sitting continues for at least two minutes so that the subjects' eyes adjust to the darkness.

**4.** The tester instructs the subjects to look down in the general direction of the piled hands. He flashes the lamp for *no more than a second*, illuminating the hands against the black towel.

**5.** The subjects slowly remove their hands from the circle but keep their eyes fixed to where they saw the hands.

**Results & Conclusions**

In about 5 seconds, a ghostly white 3-D image of the piled hands appeared in the darkness. Subjects were invited to move their real hands to touch the "ghost" hands—an eerie experience! The image turned pink, green, then faded to blue before it disappeared.

As hypothesized, the sudden flash of white light from the desk lamp triggered the light and color sensitive cells in our eyes. These cells produce *rhodopsin*—electrochemical signals that carry information to the brain even after the light went out. (Rhodopsin is a red photosensitive pigment in the retinal rods that is important for vision in dim light. Most marine fishes and higher vertebrates have rhodopsin.) The continued firing of rhodopsin-producing cells produced the positive afterimage of ghostly hands.

Light-sensitive cells coat the inner wall of the eye called the retina. The cells are of two types, rods and cones. Rods evolved for night vision because they are sensitive to shades of gray. Cones evolved for day vision because they sense color. The afterimage of hands changed color because the red and green cones stopped firing before the blue cones stopped, allowing the hands to fade to blue. The afterimage was three-dimensional because, just as when we see, the brain assembled the two afterimages into one three-dimensional image.

Since the rods and cones were accustomed to several minutes of darkness, shocking them with a sudden burst of light created such an excess of rhodopsin that it took several minutes before the normal chemistry of the eyes was restored.

# Rosemary & Number Recall

*Does smelling the herb rosemary improve number recall?*

## Materials
- 6 sprigs fresh rosemary (dried is OK, but fresh is better)
- 6 index cards and marker
- 6 friends (3 males and 3 females) as test subjects

## Background
Since ancient times, the herb rosemary *(Rosmarinus officinalis)* has been thought to improve memory. The small evergreen shrub was used by the ancient Egyptians not only as a preservative but as a sacred herb that would help the embalmed remember those left behind. The Romans also believed rosemary improved memory. Roman students massaged rosemary oil into their foreheads before taking examinations. And in medieval times, rosemary was considered a love charm that would help a couple remember their wedding vows. Paintings of the time show that the herb was sometimes made into a wreath for the bride's head.

    This project seeks to test whether the scent of rosemary can actually improve short-term memory as measured by a number-recollection test.

## Procedure
Subjects are read number sequences of increasing length and try to repeat the sequences from memory. Subjects are then given a sprig of rosemary, instructed to sniff it, and are read a different set of sequences which they try to repeat. Tests results are compared.

## Hypothesis
The subjects will perform better after smelling the rosemary.

## Experiment to Test Hypothesis
**1.** The tester writes a sequence of 4, 5, and 6 numbers on three index cards. This is the first set. He makes a copy of this set with the same numbers in a different order.

**2.** The tester writes a sequence of 7, 8, and 9 numbers on another three index cards. This is the second set. He makes a copy of this set with the same numbers in a different order.

**3.** Before receiving rosemary, subjects are tested individually by being read each index card from the original first set. After the card is read, subjects are asked to repeat the sequence of numbers back to the tester who grades for accuracy.

**4.** Step 3 is repeated, this time with cards from the original second set.

**5.** Each subject receives a sprig of rosemary (or a pinch of it in a folded paper) and is instructed to crush it and smell it.

**6.** The tester repeats Steps 3 and 4, but this time with the copies of each set of index cards.

**7.** Results for the two tests are compared for accuracy.

## Results & Conclusions

To minimize the effect aging can have on memory, it was important that our subjects were all about the same age—in this case, all 12 year olds. Three were females and three were males. It was also important that subjects had not used a scent of any kind or consumed food in the past hour. Subjects were asked to wash their hands before the test.

Since the ability to recall a number is influenced by the number's position on the list (first and last numbers being the easiest to remember), we factored in that the first and last numbers would be the most accurately remembered. Each subject was tested individually, out of sight and sound of other subjects, and subjects were allowed a 1-minute break between the tests.

When the subjects used rosemary, their recall seemed considerably improved. This was reflected in each subject's recalling more numbers from the longer sequences in the second set. All subjects could recall the number sequences in the first set—both with and without rosemary. However, without rosemary, only one subject could recall 8 numbers in sequence from the second set. After smelling the rosemary, five subjects correctly repeated 8 numbers in the second set, and one recalled all 9 numbers.

Subjects reported that they enjoyed the scent of the rosemary and that it helped relax them during the test. It may be that relaxation alone is enough for the brain to do its best remembering.

# Sense Transference in the Brain

*Does a subject temporarily deprived of sight develop a keener sense of touch? If so, does it vanish when the subject's sight is restored?*

## Materials
- blindfold
- clock to time intervals between tests
- marking pen
- tape
- shallow shirt box with one side cut out
- 3 friends as test subjects
- 4-inch-square (10-cm-square) sample of these CAMI-grade sandpapers

    C500, particle size 19.7 microns (0.00077 inches)
    C600, particle size 16.0 microns (0.00062 inches)
    C800, particle size 12.2 microns (0.00048 inches)
    C1000, particle size 9.2 microns (0.00036 inches)
    C1200, particle size 6.5 microns (0.00026 inches)
    C1500, particle size 3.2 microns (0.00012 inches)

**Note:** *CAMI stands for Coated Abrasives Manufacturers' Institute, a grading standard for sandpapers. The particle size is measured in microns. If it's difficult to obtain CAMI grades at your local hardware store, select the six finest grades available. For this project, the grit size is less important than the similarity of textures among the samples.*

*25,000 microns = 1 inch (or 2.5 cm)*

## Background
Scientists who study the brain have long suspected that the loss of one sense can enhance another. New research has provided better evidence that, specifically, the loss of sight can be compensated for with a keener sense of touch. Although such neurological flexibility was once only considered a feature of a developing brain, scientists now understand that these so-called plastic interactions exist in the adult brain as well.

At the University of Rome (Italy), a test devised by Doctor Salvatore Aglioti asked 28 subjects to place their fingers on a glass plate etched with fine grooves. While sighted, the test subjects had difficulty distinguishing between the finest grooves on the glass, if they could feel them at all. But after 90 minutes in a blindfold, the same subjects could correctly detect and identify the most minute scratches. Repeating the test 150 minutes after the blindfolds were removed, the same subjects could no longer identify the grooves accurately because their sense of touch had "reset" itself to normal.

This project will attempt to reproduce the results of that test with three test subjects and six different grades of fine sandpaper.

## Procedure

Six samples of sandpaper are taped to a table in front of a test subject. A shallow shirt box with one side removed is placed over the samples so that subjects can't see the samples they will feel. Out of sight from the others, each subject is invited to reach under the box and explore the samples with their fingertips. Subjects are then asked to rate the sandpapers from fine to coarse.

After spending 90 minutes in blindfolds, the subjects are invited to touch and rate the samples again. This time the order of the samples is changed and the box covering isn't necessary. Subjects remove blindfolds after this test.

After 150 minutes, the sighted subjects are asked to repeat the first test with a box covering the reordered samples. The results from all three touch tests are compared.

## Hypothesis

The outcome of this project should support recent evidence that the loss of sight can be replaced by the keener sense of touch, and that this keener sense of touch will revert back to normal once sight is restored.

## Experiment to Test Hypothesis

**1.** Cut each grade of sandpaper into 4-inch-square (10-cm-square) pieces. Number the pieces 1 through 6, with the lower numbers indicating the finest grades of sandpaper.

**2.** For the first test, decide on what order to place your sandpaper samples. Write it down.

**3.** Tape the six sandpaper samples to the surface of the table in a row.

**4.** Cut off one side of a shallow shirt box and place it over the samples.

**5.** Invite the first test subject to come in, reach under the box, and (with the fingers of both hands) count the six samples arranged in a row. By memorizing this spatial relationship, the tester should be able to "read" the samples from left to right and identify their relative fineness or coarseness by calling out a number between 1 and 6.

**6.** Repeat Step 5 with the second subject, and then the third. Remember to record how each subject rates the samples.

**7.** Blindfold the subjects and wait 90 minutes. (This would be a good time to invite them to take a snooze!) After 90 minutes, reorder your sandpaper samples and invite the first subject to come in and repeat the test, this time with the box covering removed. Record the results and remove the blindfolds from your subjects.

**8.** Wait another 150 minutes, reorder the samples a third time, and repeat the test with the box covering. Compare all test results among the three subjects.

## Results & Conclusions

As expected, the results of the project supported the hypothesis that one sense can compensate for the loss of another sense. In this case, each subject experienced a keener sense of touch following a 90-minute period of temporary, artificially induced (blindfold) blindness.

For the first test, not one of the three subjects correctly identified the order of fineness among the sandpaper samples. The best performer—Subject #2—was able to distinguish between the two coarsest papers only. The other subjects ordered the papers incorrectly, even confusing the finest sandpapers with the least fine.

After spending 90 minutes in blindfolds, the subjects' sense of touch improved dramatically for the second test. The best performer—Subject #2—ordered all but one of the reshuffled samples in the correct sequence. The remaining subjects got about half of them correct, slipping up on the very fine grades of paper. This was still a noticeable improvement.

After 1½ hours and with blindfolds removed, the subjects once again had trouble distinguishing grades of fineness among samples. Having had their sight restored for this third test, the subjects' sense of touch appeared to have reverted back to normal. These results successfully replicated Doctor Aglioti's test results and support evidence of sense transference in the brain.

# Simulate Neuropathic Pain

*Is it possible to simulate neuropathic pain in an otherwise healthy individual by inducing the thermal-grill illusion?*

## Materials
- 3 identical knives with metal handles (blunt dinner knives, not steak or carving knives)
- 2 drinking glasses (same size)
- warm water from tap
- cold water with ice cubes
- clock with second hand
- friend to help
- adult helper

**Caution:** *Always be very careful when handling knives.*

## Background
Millions of people throughout the world experience a disorder called neuropathic pain. For people with this affliction, even a cool breeze can trigger painful burning sensations on the skin. Although the deeper mysteries of this condition are yet to be unraveled, neurologists have named it the *thermal-grill illusion.* They believe that the most likely explanation of the illusion is that some confusion in the nerve circuitry of the body allows certain "wrong" signals to override "right" signals and reach the brain first.

A breakthrough in this understanding came when neurologists recognized that some nerves carry signals much faster than others, and that "fast" and "slow" nerves are each associated with specific sensations.

## Procedure
A thermal-grill illusion is induced in two places on the body—the back of the wrist and on the lips. The instrument used is a chilled knife handle bundled with two warm knife handles.

## Hypothesis
Wrist and lips will feel a brief but harmless stinging sensation when the bundled knife handles are applied.

## Experiment to Test Hypothesis
**1.** Fill one of the two drinking glasses with cold water and ice cubes and place one of the knives, handle side down, into the glass.

**2.** Run tap water from the faucet until it's very warm but not painfully hot. Fill the second glass with the warm water and place the other two knives in it. Leave the knives in the warm water for 60 seconds.

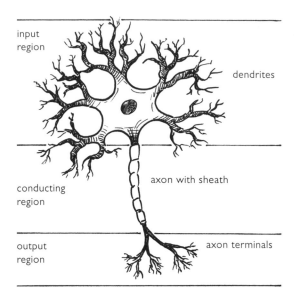

**input region**

**dendrites**

**conducting region**

**axon with sheath**

**output region**

**axon terminals**

**Nerve Cell**

**3.** Ask your helper to remove all the knives from the water and place the cold knife snugly between the two warm knives.

**4.** Close your eyes and have your helper quickly touch the three handles to the inside of your wrist. Note the sensation.

**5.** Repeat Steps 1 through 3, but this time ask your helper to place the three handles to your lips. Compare this sensation to the previous one.

**Results & Conclusions**

When the three knife handles were applied to the inside of our wrists, we experienced a stinging sensation something along the lines of a burning pinprick. The pain seemed unrelated to either heat or cold. This sensory confusion occurs because several types of nerves are stimulated at once. These nerves all compete for the same neural pathways, and only some of them will reach the brain.

Cold objects touching the skin stimulate both fast-conducting nerves that signal cold and slower nerves that signal pain. These fast and slow nerves connect to the same place in the spinal cord where the information is passed to the brain. Since the faster nerves (cold) get to the spinal cord first, they wind up blocking the slower nerves (pain). When touched by a cold object, your brain receives the message "cold!" but nothing about pain.

Adding two warm stimuli to one cold stimulus complicates this process. The warm knife handles surrounding the cold handle neutralize the cold message that the fast nerves receive. This process, called *spatial summation*, allows sensory signals to blend over a broad patch of skin. Since the fast nerves (cold) are now inactive, the slow nerves (pain) have a chance to travel to the spine and brain and deliver their signals. Suddenly, your temperature-sensing nerves aren't firing, and your pain nerves are. The result is a message to the brain that says "Ouch!"

Touching the knives to the lips produced another sensation, much more complex. Here, warm and cold sensations alternated and there was no pain involved. Unlike the skin of the wrist, the lips do not experience spatial summation and lump together stimuli from a single patch of skin. This means that lips—as many people already know—were made to feel much finer sensory details.

# Three

# MAGNET
# Madness

# Aluminum Air Battery

*Is it possible to produce useful amounts of power from an inexpensive, nontoxic, and recyclable material like aluminum?*

## Materials

- 12x16-inch (30x15-cm) sheet aluminum foil
- activated charcoal (for aquarium filters)
- two 1-foot (30-cm) lengths of electrical wire
- 2 alligator clips
- 6-volt flashlight bulb
- flashlight bulb socket
- paper towel
- small bowl
- salt
- warm water

## Background

Concern about the environment has encouraged scientists to develop alternative sources of energy. Batteries, although an improvement over fossil fuels, are hardly the answer. Conventional batteries are large, heavy, use toxic materials (that must be disposed of), and aren't powerful enough for many everyday tasks, such as driving a vehicle over long distances. Environmental considerations are not the only reason scientists are working hard to come up with a better battery design. Useful batteries must not only be portable and clean, they must also satisfy the demand for peak power over longer periods.

Aluminum might be the answer. It's recyclable, easily stored, noncombustible, and it holds a lot of energy. A battery powered by aluminum is not only simple to design, clean to run, and inexpensive to produce, but it can be made small enough to fit into any device. Aluminum is also efficient. Recent studies suggest that, compared to lithium-ion and nickel-cadmium batteries, the aluminum-powered battery provides almost 75 times more energy output over a longer battery lifetime.

A simple aluminum *air* battery—so-called because of the reactive potential of aluminum and air—will be constructed and tested in this project.

## Procedure

An aluminum air battery is constructed out of aluminum foil, paper towel, saltwater, and aquarium-filter charcoal. The battery is tested on a 6-volt flashlight bulb.

## Hypothesis

The battery will successfully demonstrate an environmentally "clean" way to produce electrical current.

## Experiment to Test Hypothesis

**1.** Fill the small bowl with warm water and stir in salt until no more salt dissolves. The salty water will be the electrical conducting fluid, or *electrolyte*, of the battery.

**2.** Place the sheet of aluminum on a flat surface you don't mind getting a little wet. Tear off a piece of paper towel, twice the size of the aluminum, and put it in the salt water.

**3.** Remove the soaked paper towel from the bowl and place it on the aluminum foil, doubling it over. Make sure the towel completely covers the foil.

**4.** Pour 1 cup (240 ml) of activated charcoal over the folded paper towel, and smooth the charcoal into a layer about 1 centimeter (about ⅜ inch) thick.

**5.** Attach an alligator clip to a piece of wire and place the clip end of the wire right in the center of the charcoal. Attach the other alligator clip to the second piece of wire. Attach that clip to an edge of the aluminum foil.

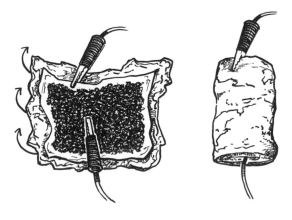

**6.** Roll the aluminum foil and paper towel into a kind of flattened burrito shape. Attach the ends of the wires to the screws of the flashlight bulb socket.

**7.** Gently push down on the aluminum and observe the bulb. Release pressure and observe the bulb again, noting results.

## Results & Conclusions

Pressing down on the aluminum caused a crunching sound as the charcoal crushed against itself in the aluminum foil. Pressing down also caused the bulb to glow brightly. Releasing pressure on the aluminum caused the bulb to go out. It was clear that this battery produced current by the action of pressing down. And it continued to light our bulb after nearly 15 minutes of continuous testing!

The battery's power was produced through a simple electrochemical reaction between the water-soaked aluminum and the oxygen. Electricity was produced as the aluminum oxidized. In our model, the activated charcoal, filled with gas pockets, provided a concentrated source of oxygen in an electrically conducting medium—carbon. Pushing down on the charcoal released oxygen and lowered the electrical resistance of the charcoal, allowing the current to flow. This reaction could happen only in an aqueous solution of salt water.

To "recharge" our aluminum battery, we needed only to replace the aluminum foil. Since aluminum is economical, easily produced, and recyclable, this project shows that it's possible to produce useful amounts of power from nontoxic and reusable materials.

# Cellular Phone EMR & Topography

*What topographical conditions affect the distribution of electromagnetic radiation (EMR) in a cellular-phone (wireless or mobile phone) network?*

## Materials
- cell phone
- friend with cell phone
- wristwatch with second hand
- map of your area
- notebook (to log results)

## Background
Cell phones use radio signals that are received and transmitted through communication towers, each of which services a small zone called a cell. Cell-phone towers are distributed all over the country. Just as an airplane passes from one air-traffic-control tower to another, a cell phone is handed off from one communication tower to the next as it moves through an area's cells.

Cell phones have low-power transmitters in them. Although most car phones have a transmitter power of 3 watts, a handheld cell phone operates on about 0.75 to 1 watt of power. The radio waves that send the encoded signal are made up of electromagnetic radiation. The function of an antenna in any radio transmitter is to launch these radio waves into space; in the case of cell phones, these waves are picked up by a receiver in the cell-phone tower.

Electromagnetic radiation is made up of waves of energy moving at the speed

of light (186,000 miles [300,000 km] per second). These waves can be bent, deflected, focused, or even blocked, depending on certain geographical conditions which this project seeks to identify.

## Procedure
Over the course of a week, calls are made from multiple locations to a stationary location. The calls are made at the same time of day to control variables and attempt to isolate the topographical conditions that affect the quality of coverage. Coverage quality is rated according to how quickly the connection is made, the general clarity of the participants' voices, and the consistency of signal (no breaking up).

## Hypothesis

Coverage will vary according to certain topographical features—yet to be identified —present in the initiating caller's location.

## Experiment to Test Hypothesis

**1.** Over the course of a week, coordinate a daily two-minute call time with a friend. Morning is best, since later in the day increased radio-wave "traffic" from other devices can degrade your connection and skew your results.

**2.** Find a local map of your area and choose seven locations from which to make your calls. The locations should vary from day to day—the first near buildings, the second among trees, the third in an open area, the fourth from a high place, the fifth from a low place, and so on.

**3.** Rate the quality of the cell-phone signal on a scale of 1 to 10, with the higher number indicating a better signal. Write the numbers on the map and compare areas for quality of signal. Note any connections between the topography of an area and the quality of signal strength.

## Results & Conclusions

After only three days of testing, it became clear that several topographical factors influenced the quality of a cell-phone signal. The largest obstacle was in the form of buildings, and calls made from downtown areas—particularly on streets bordered by tall buildings—were the poorest in quality and were rated between 1 and 4. Stepping into a building sometimes disconnected the caller completely, although this wasn't always the case. Interestingly, although we were never able to obtain a reliable signal from a ground-floor elevator, the signal grew in strength and was very robust if the elevator ascended to the top of the building. Obviously, signal strength increases with height since higher places have fewer obstacles. Signals from a rooftop or the higher floors of a building generally received a connection-quality rating of 8.

Trees were effective blockers of cell-phone signals. A call made from the wooded section of a local park received a connection-quality rating of only 6. This rating improved to 10 when, on the next day, the call was made from an open field area of the park. The following day, a call was made from a drainage culvert cut through a shallow valley. The signal strength was very poor here—with a rating of only 3, and a complete disconnect after only 40 seconds of communication.

But surprisingly, the most effective signal blackout of all occurred in an unlikely place—a basketball court completely enclosed by an aluminum chain-link cage. Even a weak signal couldn't survive within the cage, although walking out of the court and back to the street restored some level of coverage. This unusual result was supported by the fact that aluminum cages are often used to shield certain sensitive devices from radio signals. Grounded aluminum screens are often used in hospitals to protect sensitive computers from potentially damaging interference from other electronic devices.

# Cellular Phone EMR & Weather

*What atmospheric conditions affect cell-phone reception?*

## Materials
- cell phone
- friend with cell phone
- wristwatch with second hand
- notebook to log results
- pen

## Background
Unlike land lines, cellular phones (what we call cell phones, mobile phones, or wireless phones) use radio signals that are received and transmitted through communication towers. These towers are distributed all over the country, and each tower services a small zone called a "cell." A typical cell is about 10 square miles, but cells can be bigger or smaller depending on the population or needs of an area.

Since cell phones are basically transmitters, they emit radio waves in the form of radio-frequency (RF) energy, a form of electromagnetic radiation (EMR). The function of a cell phone's antenna is to launch this radiation into space where it can be picked up by the receiver in the cell phone tower.

Electromagnetic radiation is made up of waves of energy moving at the speed of light (186,000 miles [300,000 kilometers] per second). These waves can be bent, deflected, focused, or dispersed according to certain environmental conditions which this project seeks to identify.

## Procedure
A cell phone call is made to the same location from the same location in various types of weather and at different times of days to see what conditions affect reception. Success is rated according to how quickly the connection is made and the clarity of the call.

## Hypothesis
The quality of reception will vary according to weather and time of day the call is made.

## Experiment to Test Hypothesis
**1.** Over the course of a week, coordinate three daily call times with a friend—morning, noon, and early evening. If possible, you should both agree to make and receive calls from the same location each day.

**2.** Before making your first call, keep a log of the time and weather. Allow it to continue for about two minutes. Rate the quality of the call not only on how quickly you connect, but on the general clarity of your friend's voice and consistency of signal (no breaking up).

**3.** Repeat Step 2 in the afternoon and evening (for five weekdays and two weekend days). Log your results and compare them.

## Results & Conclusions

Two of the seven days we had cloudiness and rain. On these days (Tuesday and Wednesday) the cell-phone connection generally took longer and the signal strength wasn't as reliable. Of the two cloudy and rainy days, we found much more static behind our friend's voice and considerably more breaking up of the signal when it rained. Although this is what we might've expected from a land line, it came as a bit of a surprise from a cell phone.

The behavior of RF energy explains the poorer signal. Radio waves are slowed or even blocked by obstacles, and a thicker, precipitating atmosphere provides a less transparent environment for transmission. Unlike sound waves, which are amplified and carried farther by moisture in the air, radio waves—particularly those in the lower frequencies—are slowed down and scattered. Clear, dry, sunny weather seemed to markedly improve the cell-phone signal.

This correlation-with-weather hypothesis was only partially correct, however. The most pronounced difference in connection quality seemed to have more to do with when the call was made rather than the kind of weather that prevailed. For example, weekday calls made at 7 A.M. connected quickly and were of generally good quality. Calls made at noon took longer to connect, but also sounded good. The biggest difference occurred around 5 o'clock in the evening. These calls not only took longer to connect, but the quality of the connection was degraded by static, breaking up, and occasional disconnects.

The reason for these differences probably had to do with increased electromagnetic interference (EMI) from other devices (including other cell phones) at peak times of day. This kind of traffic, or EMI "pollution," as some have called it, makes using a cell phone at certain times of day unreliable. Interference due to high traffic was noticeable only during the weekdays of the testing period. On both Saturday and Sunday, cell-phone reception was generally clear.

# Detecting Magnetite

*How can we prove that a magnetic form of iron exists in soil?*

## Materials
- container for soil
- small bowl
- tablespoon
- glass pie dish
- neodymium magnet (from science supply store)
- cellophane wrap
- cotton swab (Q-tip)

## Background
Iron is one of Earth's most plentiful resources, making up at least 5% of its crust. However, some of this iron is in the form of magnetite, a naturally magnetic substance. The transformation of nonmagnetic iron into magnetite is due to the eating habits of a type of soil bacteria called *hyperthermophiles*, meaning "those that love hot temperatures."

Since iron was abundant in the newly formed Earth long before plant forms evolved, scientists now believe that these primitive heat-loving organisms were among the first forms of life. This is supported by the fact that some of the oldest geological sites in the world also have the highest concentrations of magnetite.

## Procedure
One tablespoon (15 ml) of ordinary soil is mixed into a bowl of water. A magnet wrapped in cellophane is dipped into the soil mixture to attract particles. If particles are found, they're tested to see if they are mutually attractive, indicating magnetite.

## Hypothesis
We should find traces of magnetite in ordinary soil.

## Experiment to Test Hypothesis

**1.** Collect some soil in a container.

**2.** Place 1 tablespoon (15 ml) of soil into a bowl of water and stir it around.

**3.** Wrap the neodymium magnet in a piece of cellophane and dip it several times into the soil and water mixture. Notice how particles of soil stick to the cellophane.

**4.** Dip the cellophane-wrapped magnet into a pie plate filled with clear water and carefully remove the magnet from the cellophane. The particles will drop away from the cellophane and settle at the bottom of the pie plate.

**5.** Bring the magnet close to the surface of the water and slowly move it. The particles will follow the magnet, proving that they are made of iron.

**6.** Dip the cotton swab into the water and push the particles together. They will clump, showing that they are magnetic magnetite and attracted to each other.

## Results & Conclusions

A substantial quantity of magnetite exists in soil. Not only was the magnetite attracted to the strong neodymium magnet, but each particle attracted other particles, proving its naturally magnetic attributes.

# Fast & Slow Magnets

*What effect does a magnet have on three different materials?*

---

## Materials
- 3-foot (90-cm) iron pipe
- four 18-inch (45-cm) cardboard wrapping-paper tubes
- duct tape
- aluminum foil
- neodymium magnet (available at science supply stores)

## Background
Physicists tell us that magnets affect all types of materials, even those that fail to display a noticeable attraction to the magnet. Magnetic attraction can be classified into three types: *ferromagnetism* (an attraction to iron, cobalt, and nickel), *paramagnetism* (electrical current created in the presence of copper and aluminum), and *diamagnetism* (weak repulsion in the presence of nonmetals).

Of the three, paramagnetism has been the most interesting to physicists because it links magnetism to electricity. In the nineteenth century, the scientist Michael Faraday first demonstrated that an electrical current could be created in a copper wire by moving a magnet against it. This principle, called *induction*, helped create the first electromagnetic generator. Physicists now understand that induction can be created in other metals such as aluminum. They also understand more about induction—how moving a magnet against a metal like aluminum creates electrical "eddy currents" in the aluminum that have a noticeable effect on the magnet.

## Procedure
The neodymium magnet is dropped through three tubes of different materials—iron, cardboard, and cardboard wrapped in aluminum foil— and the speeds of each drop are compared.

## Hypothesis
The magnet will be attracted to the iron pipe, stick to it, and not drop through. The magnet will not be attracted to the cardboard tube and drop through. The magnet will not be attracted to the aluminum-covered tube and drop through, since induction is not an attractive force.

## Experiment to Test Hypothesis

**1.** Use the duct tape to attach two cardboard wrapping tubes into a tube 3 feet (90 cm) long. Attach the second set of tubes the same way.

**2.** Wrap one of the cardboard tubes in several layers of aluminum foil, taping the foil where necessary.

**3.** Hold the iron pipe vertically and drop the magnet through one end. The magnet sticks to the wall of the pipe and will not drop through.

**4.** Hold the cardboard tube vertically and drop the magnet through. The magnet passes straight through the tube and falls out the other end.

**5.** Hold the aluminum-wrapped tube and drop the magnet through. The magnet passes through the tube, but slowly, and drops out of the other end.

## Results & Conclusions

Our hypothesis was incorrect in stating that induction would not affect the drop-rate of the magnet through the aluminum-covered tube. The fact that the magnet fell slowly indicates the presence of electrical eddy currents created in the foil, which acted to slow the descent of the magnet through the tube. This is why a paramagnetic phenomenon like induction can be used for electrical braking systems, spinning the dials on gauges, speedometers, and similar devices where an electrical "air-bag" effect is necessary.

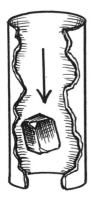 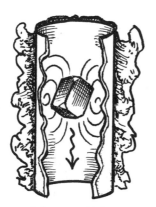

unwrapped tube          foil-wrapped tube

# Minuscule Motor

Adult Help Required

*Can a working motor be made simply enough to demonstrate reversing polarity and other important concepts of electromagnetism?*

## Materials

- alkaline D-cell battery
- battery holder for D-cell
- used AAA battery
- neodymium magnet or similar rare-earth magnet (from science or electronics store)
- 22-gauge enamel-coated magnet wire
- 18-gauge or 20-gauge plastic-coated electrical wire
- paper
- craft knife
- scissors

**Caution:** *Using a craft knife to strip away wire insulation can be difficult. Make sure that an adult assists you.*

## Background

One of the most important applications of electromagnetic force over the past 200 years has been in the design of the reversing-polarity armature—better known as the *rotary motor.* Physicists as early as Michael Faraday (1791–1867) invented simple motors based on the principle that magnetic fields could be created, manipulated, and turned into mechanical motion. Without the electric motor, our modern technological age could not exist. Motors drive all sorts of machines, both stationary and mobile.

Motors make *automation* possible—the backbone of our mechanized, industrial society.

The workings of even the most complicated electric motor can be reduced to one simple principle: like poles of a magnet repel and unlike poles attract. In the case of a motor's turning part, or *armature*, the magnet is actually an electromagnet—a magnetic field produced by a current of electricity. This electromagnetic field interacts with the magnetic field of a permanent (nonelectromagnetic) magnet placed near the armature. The interplay of both magnetic fields produces the turning motion of the motor.

**D-Cell Battery**

This project seeks to construct a simple motor where the above principles are clearly demonstrated. Our motor will be very small, hardly practical, but certainly fun to watch.

## Procedure
Wire, battery, and a neodymium magnet are combined to make a tiny working motor operated by a simple interrupt switch.

## Hypothesis
The motor will spin despite its minimal design.

## Experiment to Test Hypothesis
1. To make the armature, wind the magnet wire about 20 times around a used AAA battery. Wind it tight so that you have a good coil, but leave about 2 inches (5 cm) of straight wire on each side of the coil.

2. Remove the coil from the battery. Loop the straight wires around the coil so that you make two knots, exactly opposite each other. These knots must be exactly parallel since the straight wires will form an axle on which the coil will rotate.

3. Hold the coil at the edge of a table so that the coil stands vertically (not flat) and one of the straight wires lies flat on the table surface. Use the craft knife to carefully scrape the top half of the wire to remove the enamel insulation. The bottom half of the wire should keep its insulation. Do the same for the other wire.

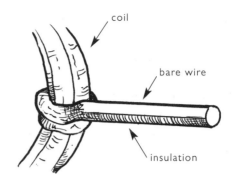

4. To make the axle supports, cut the electrical wire into two 4-inch (10-cm) pieces and use the craft knife to strip the plastic from the wire. Take one wire and wrap its center around a nail, making a small loop. Repeat this for the other paper wire.

5. Attach the wire supports to the battery holder by winding their ends through the small holes at each end of the holder. Bend the supports apart slightly and insert the axle into both rings. Bend the rings back so that they're close to the coil but not touching it.

6. Cut the paper into a small strip. While holding the strip over the flat terminal of the D-cell battery, put the battery into the holder. The strip of paper acts as an interrupt switch for the motor.

7. Place the neodymium magnet on top of the battery holder just underneath the coil. Make sure the magnet's pole points up. Also make sure that the coil spins freely and clears the magnet.

**8.** To start the motor, remove the paper strip. If nothing happens, spin the armature gently to overcome any initial friction. If it still doesn't move, coax the armature in the other direction.

## Results & Conclusions

With only a little push to start it, the armature spun in a clockwise direction. Electricity flowed up one support into the armature, then back down the other support and into the battery again. But this happened only when the scraped half of the wire faced down, touching the supports. When the insulated half faced down, contact was broken and no current flowed.

But an interrupted current made for a spinning motor. Here's how: When current flowed through the wire, the armature became an electromagnet with north and south poles. The electromagnet's north and south poles were attracted or repelled by the corresponding poles on the neodymium magnet.

When we scraped off the insulation from the armature axles, we did it with the coil standing up, and not lying flat on the table. This made the poles of the electromagnet point to the left and right (as if the coil were wrapped around an invisible permanent magnet). If the coil had been flat on the table when we scraped the wire, the poles would have pointed up and down.

Since the electromagnet's poles pointed left and right, they had to rotate in order to line up with the up and down poles of the permanent magnet underneath. So the coil turned to line up with the magnet. But once that happened, the enameled half of the wire touched the supports, cutting off the current. No electricity meant that the coil was no longer an electromagnet. This left it free to coast around until the scraped half touched the support, electrical current resumed, and the whole rotational process got another kick forward.

# Repulsive Prunes

*Is it possible to demonstrate diamagnetic repulsion with the aid of two wet prunes and a strong magnet?*

## Materials
- 2 dried prunes (from a can, box, or plastic container)
- plastic drinking straw
- 2 feet (60 cm) of thread
- cellophane tape
- neodymium magnet (available at science supply stores)
- table edge (to hang thread from)

## Background
Experiments demonstrating diamagnetism have become easier to assemble nowadays due to the availability of novelty supermagnets such as neodymium. Just about everyone has seen the old iron-filings-on-a-bar demonstrations. Projects involving diamagnetism are new and different.

Magnetic attraction can be classified into three types: *ferromagnetism* (an attraction to iron, cobalt, and nickel), *paramagnetism* (electrical current created in the presence of copper and aluminum), and *diamagnetism*—the most mysterious of all. Diamagnetic materials include bismuth, silver, gold, carbon-graphite, diamond, water, protein, and even DNA.

Diamagnetism gets its antimagnetic reputation because when diamagnetic materials are exposed to a magnetic field, they induce a weak magnetic field in the opposite direction, so that their magnetic susceptibility is *negative*. This means that diamagnetic materials are repulsed by either pole of a strong magnet and move away from it. But what makes diamagnetism really exciting is that it's the natural "magnetic" state of much of the non-magnetic world—including the human body.

This project uses something less complicated than the human body to demonstrate diamagnetism—two canned prunes.

## Procedure
Two prunes are attached to the opposite sides of a plastic straw that is balanced on a string. A neodymium magnet is placed close to one of the prunes and the results observed.

## Hypothesis
The prune close to the magnet will rotate away from the magnet, demonstrating the diamagnetic properties of water, sugar, and prune tissue.

## Experiment to Test Hypothesis

**1.** Find an area without air turbulence. Even a slight breeze can ruin the results of your experiment.

**2.** Use the prong of a fork to make a hole in each prune. Push the prunes onto the ends of the straw.

**3.** Tie one end of the thread to the middle of the straw (or at a spot close to middle) so that the prunes will be perfectly balanced.

**4.** Tape the other end of the thread to the side of a table or back of a chair so that the prunes can hang freely. Allow the prunes to twist for awhile until they appear perfectly still.

**5.** Bring one pole of the neodymium magnet close to a prune. Don't touch the prune with the magnet.

**6.** Turn the magnet around and bring the other pole close to a prune. Observe the results.

## Results & Conclusions

Supporting our hypothesis, the prune was repelled by both poles of the neodymium magnet and rotated away from the magnet. The effect was dramatic and probably would've been noticeable even in a breezy area. The properties of a prune—water, sugar, and cellular material—all demonstrated their clear diamagnetic tendencies through this project.

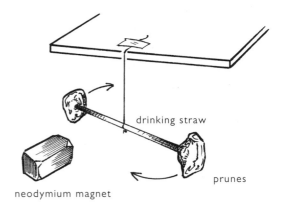

Prunes repelling a neodymium magnet.

# Strange Water

*Is water attracted to a magnet?*

## Materials
- small glass with straight sides
- isopropyl alcohol (rubbing alcohol)
- vegetable oil
- water
- eyedropper
- neodymium magnet (available at science supply stores)

## Background
Physicists tell us that magnets affect all types of materials, even those that don't display a noticeable attraction to the magnet. Magnetic attraction can be classified into three types: *ferromagnetism* (an attraction to iron, cobalt, and nickel), *paramagnetism* (electrical current created in the presence of copper and aluminum), and the most mysterious of all—*diamagnetism*.

When diamagnetic materials are exposed to a magnetic field, they induce a weak magnetic field in the opposite direction, so that their magnetic susceptibility is *negative*. This means that diamagnetic materials are repulsed by either pole of a strong magnet and move away from it.

Diamagnetic materials include bismuth, silver, gold, carbon-graphite, diamond, water, protein, and even DNA. Bismuth and carbon-graphite are the strongest, around 20 times more diamagnetic than water.

## Procedure
Oil drops are suspended between layers of water and alcohol. A strong magnet is placed against the glass next to the oil drops and the result observed.

## Hypothesis
Although water is diamagnetic, the repulsion effect of the magnet is so subtle that it will not have any noticeable effect on the oil drops.

## Experiment to Test Hypothesis
**1.** Fill a small glass two-thirds full with isopropyl alcohol.

**2.** Using the eyedropper, add 10 drops of vegetable oil to the glass and observe how the drops sink to the bottom of the alcohol.

**3.** Slowly add water to the glass. The water will slip to the bottom of the glass so that the alcohol containing the oil drops will float above. Add just enough water so that the oil drops are suspended between the water and alcohol layers.

**4.** Place the magnet on a stack of books against the glass so that a magnetic pole touches the area where the oil drops are suspended.

**5.** Add 5 more drops of oil; then wait a few minutes and record the result.

### Results & Conclusions

The hypothesis was incorrect, perhaps due to the strength of the neodymium magnet. After only a few minutes, it was apparent that the oil drops were combining into one large drop that moved to the edge of the glass where the magnet was. Although at first this result suggested that the oil was magnetic, what actually happened was that the water was driven away (repulsed) by the magnet, and the oil drops combined and moved into the area left by the moving water. This repulsion of water from a strong magnet demonstrates the principle of diamagnetism.

# Four

# LOTS *of Botany*

# Dandelion Curlicues

*Can the unique water-retaining properties of a dandelion be observed by placing the quartered stem in a glass of water?*

## Materials
- mature dandelion blossom with stem
- craft knife
- newspaper
- glass
- water

**Caution:** *Using a craft knife to slice the dandelion stems can be difficult. Make sure that an adult assists you.*

## Background
Every gardener knows that dandelions are among the first weeds to appear in the springtime. A dandelion can spring up seemingly overnight and overwhelm that little piece of property you had reserved for the petunias or marigolds. Dandelions do well even when the soil is dry and not particularly plant-friendly. And when the rain comes at last, it's the dandy that gets the lion's share of the water. All these unique features are the result of several million years of plant evolution. Over the eons, dandelions got smart and toughened up.

Like others in the group of plants called *stem succulents*, dandelions store water in long cells that make up the inner walls of their stems. When these cells fill with water and become turgid, they stand up straight and provide excellent stem support for the rather top-heavy dandelion flower. The cells suck up water and can hold it for long periods of time, keeping the plant moist in a drought. So a dandelion is a kind of botanical camel—storing its moisture even when the soil is parched and other plants wither around them.

This project will demonstrate the dandelion's amazing water-storing abilities.

## Procedure
A mature dandelion blossom is plucked with its stem. Using a craft knife, we split the stem vertically into four sections. The dandelion with its quartered stem is placed in a glass of water and observed.

## Hypothesis
The divided sections of the stem will suck up water and swell together again.

## Experiment to Test Hypothesis

**1.** Cut a mature dandelion as close to the root as you can. Spread some newspaper on a flat surface and place the dandelion on the newspaper.

**2.** With an adult's help, use the craft knife to cut along the length of the stem from top to bottom, dividing the stem into four ribbons.

**3.** Place the dandelion, stem down, into a glass of water and watch what happens.

## Results & Conclusions

The hypothesis was incorrect. Rather than swell together, the four ribbons of stem immediately curled outward after making contact with the water. The curls were so tight that the stem could no longer prop up the dandelion blossom, allowing it to pivot and fall into the water.

Cell turgidity was the reason. The cells lining the inside wall of the stem became swollen with water and so elongated that they forced the shorter cells on the outside wall to bend backward in a curl. If the stem were still whole and tubular, the turgid cells would've provided structural support. But with the stem divided into ribbons, the expansive force of the swelling cells simply bent the ribbons backward—and in seconds!

# Plants & Plaster

*How do young plant roots change rock surfaces?*

## Materials
- dozen or more pea or bean seedlings (sprouts)
- dish cloth or other small cloth
- plaster of Paris
- shallow baking pan
- vegetable shortening
- water
- paper towels

**Note:** *You need to sprout about a dozen beans or peas in potting soil. You'll need to grow these ahead of time.*

## Background
Anyone who has ever hiked over granite boulders has seen that the top layers sometimes flake off. This occurs mostly when plants like lichens or mosses grow on the rock surface. Is it possible for the tiny roots of plants to splinter something as hard as granite in order to survive? Similarly, how is it possible for the roots of trees to penetrate huge boulders? In each case, it appears that a plant will send out roots in response to two powerful stimuli—gravity and water. The minerals contained in rocks will often keep water in a suspended state and the roots will burrow down to find it.

## Procedure
Some newly sprouted peas or beans are placed on a hardened slab of plaster of Paris. We cover the seedlings with a wet cloth. After a few days, the cloth is removed to see if the seedlings had any effect on the plaster.

## Hypothesis
The seedlings will begin to root into the plaster, decomposing it by splintering its surface.

## Experiment to Test Hypothesis
**1.** Coat the inside of the baking pan with vegetable shortening.

**2.** Mix the plaster with enough water to make a liquid with the consistency of thick cream. Slowly pour the plaster into the baking pan so that the surface is smooth and glassy. Allow the plaster to harden overnight.

**3.** Remove the plaster from the baking pan and place it on the towel.

**4.** Carefully remove the sprouted bean or pea seedlings and lay them out across the smooth side of the plaster. Place each seedling no closer than 2 inches (5 cm) from its neighbor.

**5.** Wet some paper towels and carefully lay them across the seedlings until the plaster is completely covered. Each day, sprinkle a little more water on the towels to keep them moist.

**6.** After about 1 week, remove the towels from the seedlings and observe the result.

**Results & Conclusions**

Removing the paper towels revealed a plaster surface that had changed considerably since the seedlings had been placed on it. Instead of a smooth glassy surface, the damp plaster was covered in fine yellow root hairs. Underneath the hairs, the surface of the plaster was flaked and cracked. Larger cracks contained more moisture and so, many of the thicker roots found them. This resulted in the cracks widening even further. All of the above observations confirmed the hypothesis that the roots would decompose the plaster.

# Potato Conservation

*When placed in potting soil, will a divided potato produce more potato plants than a whole potato?*

## Materials
- 2 small brown (Idaho or russet) potatoes
- plastic gardening flat (available in gardening stores; they're usually filled with groundcover plants)
- plastic knife
- potting soil
- string

## Background
All sorts of mysterious chemical reactions occur inside plants. For example, how does a seed know when to germinate? What makes a pea vine twist around a pole? Why do fruits ripen when placed near other ripened fruits?

Botanists believe the answers to these questions have to do with plant hormones. Hormones are chemically very sophisticated. Some, like *auxin*, can instruct a tendril to grow faster on one side, allowing it to curl around a pole. Others, like *ethalene*, trigger the ripening of fruits—even after the fruit is picked. Plant hormones can tell root cells to divide quickly so that the fine root hairs have a better chance of finding water. As this project demonstrates, hormones can even instruct a plant not to grow.

Potatoes also have hormones. The potato, which is actually a large underground stem called a *tuber*, does not have seeds but reproduces through the spuds (the eyes) on its skin. The spud is the reproductive organ of the potato. To raise potatoes, farmers cut them into pieces and bury them in mineral-rich soil.

## Procedure
Two potatoes are planted in the garden flat, one whole and the other cut into pieces. We water the flat for three weeks or until the potatoes sprout leaves. At that point, potato and pieces of potato are uncovered, examined, and compared.

## Hypothesis
The divided potato will produce stems and leaves on each piece. The whole potato will produce only one stem with leaves.

## Experiment to Test Hypothesis

**1.** Fill the gardening flat with potting soil and place it in a warm, well-lighted place.

**2.** Examine one of the potatoes for spuds. These are the small dimples on the surface of the potato.

**3.** With an adult's help, use the plastic knife to saw through the potato with the most spuds. Divide the potato several times until you have at least eight pieces.

**4.** Bury each potato piece in the gardening flat. Bury the whole potato next to it. Place a string down the middle of the flat to separate the divided-potato patch from the whole-potato patch.

**5.** Water the potatoes for about 3 weeks or until you see a proliferation of stems and leaves. (Don't try to figure out which stem belongs to what potato—just look for some healthy green.)

**6.** Dig up the potato pieces and whole potato and compare them.

## Results & Conclusions

The messiest bunch to dig up were the potato pieces without spuds. They smelled bad, hadn't produced growth of any kind, and showed visible signs of decay. In contrast, each of the pieces containing a spud sprouted a healthy potato plant with a strong stem and sturdy (if small) leaves. Every plant sprouted from the spud of the potato piece. The whole potato produced a large stem with wider leaves, but only from one spud. The rest of the spuds, at least 12 of them, remained inactive.

Something told the whole potato to "shut off" its remaining spuds. Something told each piece of potato to turn on its spud. If there were two spuds on a potato piece, only one sprouted.

If we believe what botanists believe, the whole potato produced an auxinlike hormone that traveled throughout the body of the potato. This hormone allowed only one spud to germinate and switched off all the other spuds. Because of this, the new growth will not have to share its supply of water and minerals with competing plants. This is also why the plant from the whole potato was so much larger than plants from the potato pieces.

# Raindrop Erosion

*How much difference does groundcover (plants that cover the soil) make in reducing soil erosion from rainfall?*

## Materials
- 2 shoe-box lids, shirt boxes, or similar shallow containers
- aluminum foil
- potting soil
- watering can with sprinkler (not spout) head
- 2 large pieces of white oaktag
- stopwatch or clock with second hand
- friend to watch the clock

**Note:** *You must prepare sprouting grass seed in one of the shoe-box lids ahead of time.*

## Background
If left unchecked, soil erosion from rainfall and flooding can have disastrous consequences for the environment. During a heavy rainfall, valuable topsoil is washed away, leaving harder, sandy, and less fertile undersoil. In addition, erosion can seriously destabilize the land so that sinkholes, mudslides, and other serious problems can occur.

Finally, water that runs off in flooding does not have a chance to sink into the ground and become part of the essential water table of Earth. This is why scientists have long recognized that groundcover is essential for keeping even a badly soaked terrain "knitted together" and stable.

## Procedure
Two shoe-box covers containing potting soil are subjected to a violent, watering-can "rainstorm." One of the groundcovers contains newly sprouted grass. The results of the rainstorm on the soils of the two shoe-box covers are observed and compared.

## Hypothesis
The shoe-box cover containing the grass will lose less soil than the one containing just soil.

## Experiment to Test Hypothesis
**1.** Place the two pieces of white oaktag on the floor about 5 feet (about 150 cm) apart. In the center of one piece, place the shoe-box cover containing the soil. In the center of the other piece, place the shoe-box cover containing the grass.

**2.** Fill the watering can and lift it over the soil shoe-box cover, holding it at about chest level.

**3.** Have a friend watch the clock, and at the signal, turn the watering can to a 45° angle and wave it back and forth across the shoe-box cover. Stop after 5 seconds. Observe the result.

**4.** Repeat this procedure for the grass shoe-box cover. Observe the result.

## Results & Conclusions

Soil spattered over the white oaktag in a circular area extending nearly 14 inches (about 35 cm) from the soil shoe-box cover. Only a little soil splattered over the oaktag under the grass shoe-box cover. Those splatterings were also smaller and contained less loose soil. It was clear that the grass broke the impact of the watering-can "rain" on the soil. In softening the percussive weight of water-on-soil, less erosion occurred in the shoe-box cover containing the grass. This is clearly why scientists recognize the value of planting groundcover over soil to reduce erosion.

# The Sweetest Fungicide

*Can honey—long known for its antibacterial properties—also prevent the growth of molds on bread?*

## Materials

- 3 slices of white bread
- 3 resealable plastic bags
- cotton swab
- water in spray bottle
- corn syrup
- honey

**Caution:** *This project requires growing molds in sealed plastic bags. Since some common bread molds can be highly toxic, do not open the bags. When you're finished with the project, discard them.*

## Background

Unlike bacteria, molds (or fungi) are made up of a "fruiting body" consisting of a stem and several reproducing cells. The reproducing cells produce small "seed" cells called spores. Mold spores are quite abundant in the air. So any food allowed to stand in the open soon becomes contaminated with mold if adequate moisture is present.

Like all living things, molds need certain environmental conditions in order to grow. Among these are food, water, and proper temperature. Just like humans, molds are mostly water, since all biochemical reactions necessary for life must take place in the water-based cytoplasm of the cell. Water is also critical because it prevents the mold from drying out.

Honey, a combination of plant pollen and bee enzymes, is made up of 35% protein, and contains half of all the necessary amino acids. It is a highly concentrated source of many essential nutrients, including large quantities of carbohydrates (sugars); minerals (iron, copper, manganese, silica, chlorine, calcium, potassium, sodium, phosphorus, aluminum, and magnesium); B complex vitamins; and vitamins C, D, and E. The antiseptic qualities of honey have been known for thousands of years; the ancient Egyptians used it as a salve to treat infected wounds. Although scientists disagree on exactly how honey fights bacteria, they do agree that honey has powerful *hygroscopic* properties, which means that it absorbs water and stimulates the production of white blood cells in human beings and animals. This project will test the effectiveness of honey's hygroscopic and antiseptic properties in controlling mold growth.

## Procedure

Three pieces of bread are moistened with water. We coat one piece with corn syrup, another with honey, and leave the last piece uncoated. The pieces are placed in resealable bags and observed for mold growth.

## Hypothesis
Although honey fights bacterial growth, a mold is not a bacterium and so the honey-coated slice will still allow mold to grow. But because honey absorbs water and molds require moisture, the mold growth will be less than on the other pieces of bread.

## Experiment to Test Hypothesis
**1.** Place 3 slices of white bread on a paper towel.

**2.** Spray a little water on each slice. Don't get them too wet.

**3.** Put the first slice in the resealable plastic bag and seal it.

**4.** Drizzle 1 tablespoon (15 ml) of corn syrup on the second slice, coating the surface as thoroughly as possible. Put the slice into a plastic bag and seal it.

**5.** Drizzle 1 tablespoon (15 ml) of honey on the third slice and put it into a plastic bag.

**6.** Label the plastic bags and place them in a dark, warm spot.

**7.** Observe the slices through the bags over the next few days and compare the mold growth on each.

## Results & Conclusions
After two days, the uncoated and corn-syrup slices showed traces of molds. These were mostly bluish-green (*penicillium* and *aspergillus*). The honey-coated slice showed no mold activity. In a week, the sugar and uncoated slices showed further mold activity with the appearance of blackish molds (*Alternaria alternata, Cladosporium herbarum*) and even pinkish molds (*fusarium*). The honey-coated slice now showed mold activity as well, but only in patches on the surface where the coating was uneven or lacking. Contrary to the hypothesis, it was clear that the honey was stopping the growth and reproduction of molds on the treated slice.

This made sense since it seems that no matter how long you keep honey on the shelf it doesn't "go bad" (although it might crystallize from excessive exposure to heat). From these observations, it must be true that the hygroscopic (water-absorbing) properties of honey must interrupt the cell metabolism in molds, which keeps the molds from surviving. Since cell processes involve the exchanging of nutrients through water-based cytoplasm, any substance that absorbs water will effectively dry out a cell and destroy it.

# Touchy-Feely Morning Glory

*How does a vine know when to wrap itself around a support?*

## Materials
- morning-glory or sweet-pea seeds
- small container
- potting soil
- pencil
- craft knife
- tweezers
- paper plate
- microscope
- adult helper

**Caution:** *Using a craft knife to slice the plant tendrils can be difficult. Make sure an adult assists you.*

Morning glory blossom and vine wrapping around stick.

## Background
To find water and light, plants mysteriously know in which direction to grow. This "growth intelligence" occurs in all parts of the plant—roots, stem, and leaves. Growth patterns, or *tropisms*, can take three basic forms—*hydrotropism* (toward water), *geotropism* (toward the pull of gravity), and *phototropism* (toward light). But another type of tropism occurs in plants—mostly vines—that must rely on an outside support to gain height and strength. Called *thigmotropism*, it's the response of a tendril when it touches a surface.

Botanists have much to learn about just how a plant senses its environment and adjusts to it. But there is strong evidence that light, gravity, water, and even touch induce the asymmetrical production of *auxin*, a growth regulator that triggers cell elongation and leads to growth and curvature.

## Procedure
A morning glory is sprouted in a small container until the vine is about 1 inch (2.54 cm) long. A pencil is placed next to the vine and the growth pattern of the vine observed. We slice a section of the vine away and observe it under a microscope.

## Hypothesis

At each point of contact between the vine and the pencil, the vine will wrap around the pencil. Microscopic examination will reveal a difference in cell structures in these contact areas.

## Experiment to Test Hypothesis

**1.** Place a few morning-glory seeds in a small container filled with potting soil. Keep the container moist and in a warm place out of the direct sun.

**2.** Continue watering the sprouted seeds until you have one tendril about 1 inch (2.54 cm) long. Push a pencil, sharp side down, into the soil near the tendril and observe the growth of the tendril over the next 24 hours.

**3.** Allow the tendril to continue growing for two days. Then, with an adult's help, use the craft knife to cut off the top of the tendril. Lay the cut tendril on a paper plate.

**4.** Hold the cutting with the tweezers while an adult carefully slices a small section along the inwardly curving edge of the tendril (where it touched the pencil). Slice a section from the outwardly curving side also. Finally, make a small slice from the very tip of the tendril.

**5.** Examine each slice under the microscope and record your observations.

## Results & Conclusions

As expected, at the point where the morning-glory tendril touched the pencil, it rapidly twisted itself around the pencil shaft and continued to climb. The first evidence of twist was apparent after only a few hours after contact. Over the course of two days, the tendril made three complete twists around the pencil and had climbed several inches (7 to 25 cm).

Cutting the tendril and examining slices of it under the microscope yielded some surprises. The cells along the inward and outwardly curving sides of the tendril showed distinct differences. There were many more cells along the outer walls of the tendril, which appeared responsible for pushing the curl of the tendril toward the pencil. These cells were also very long. The cells on the inward side of the pencil were smaller and more compact— almost stunted, in fact, as if they had been told to stop growing for the time being. Cells at the growing tip of the tendril were longer and resembled the cells along the outer wall of the tendril.

It was clear from these observations that the morning glory was reacting to the touch of the pencil. Botanists tell us that this occurs when plants release hormones that speed up tendril growth on one side and slow it down on the other. In this case, the result was a twist, or torque, around the pencil shaft. Thigmotropism evolved to allow plants with weak stems to grow upward. Without this ability, some vines could never compete for sunlight with taller plants having sturdier stems.

# Water Evaporation in Leaves

*Will a plant cutting germinate more quickly if the extra leaves and buds are removed?*

## Materials
- 2 cuttings from the tip of a healthy geranium plant
- 2 small flowerpots with soil
- 2 jars with openings large enough to rest the containers
- two 12x2-inch (30x5-cm) strips of cotton cloth
- scissors
- water
- cup
- Sharpie marking pen

## Background
Growing a new plant from a cutting can be difficult—even if the cutting source is a healthy geranium specimen. A plant cutting must conserve all its energy and food to concentrate on forming new roots, absorbing water, and keeping itself moist. Of these three challenges, water loss can be the most serious.

The following project examines the germination success of a cutting with all of its leaves left intact compared to a cutting where many of the leaves have been removed. The amount of water evaporation will be determined by observing the water levels in each jar.

## Procedure
We cut 2 three-leaf terminal buds of a geranium and placed them in flowerpots. A cotton wick is extended from each pot into a jar filled with water. One geranium cutting has most of its leaves removed while the other retains its leaves. The health of each cutting is observed and the water level in each jar is measured.

## Hypothesis
The cutting with most of its leaves removed will do better than the cutting with all of its leaves. The water levels in the jars will remain the same.

## Experiment to Test Hypothesis
**1.** Take a healthy geranium plant and cut 2 three-leaf terminal bud sections (the growing tips of the plant). Remove all but one leaf from one of the sections. Allow the other section to keep its leaves.

**2.** Roll each cotton strip into a wick, knotting it in several places to keep the roll tight. Push the ends of the wicks into the holes at the bottom of the flowerpots, pull the wicks through about 3 inches (7.6 cm), and fill the pots with soil.

**3.** Add 3 cups (720 ml) of water to each of the jars and place the flowerpots on top of the jars so that their wicks touch the water.

**4.** Poke a hole in the soil of one pot and insert the plucked geranium cutting. Insert the full-leaf cutting in the other pot.

**5.** Allow water to be drawn up into the wicks beneath both pots. After about an hour, make a mark on the outside of each jar to indicate the water level.

**6.** Observe the geranium cuttings over the next two weeks, observing their health, and comparing the water levels in the two jars.

**Results & Conclusions**

As expected, the geranium cutting with fewer leaves appeared healthier, with new sprouts appearing along the stem. The water level in the jar beneath it had dropped about 1 inch (2.54 cm) in a week's time. In comparison, the full-leaf geranium appeared sickly, with the larger leaves yellow and withered around the edge. Even though this cutting appeared drier, the water level in the jar beneath was nearly empty. On closer examination, it was clear that the full-leaf cutting was losing too much water through its leaves and not retaining enough water to promote the development of new roots and buds. The hypothesis was correct in stating that the plucked cutting would do better than the intact one.

# Which Trees Are the Most Flammable?

*Which trees are the most flammable and therefore the most dangerous during a wildfire?*

## Materials

- field guide to trees in your area
- chisel
- hammer
- can of Sterno
- lighter or match
- piece of chicken wire
- stopwatch or clock with second hand
- sticky labels
- marker
- barbeque tongs
- oven mitt
- ash juniper (cedar) tree bark
- eucalyptus tree bark
- peppertree tree bark
- piñon pine tree bark
- sycamore tree bark
- oak tree bark
- maple tree bark
- birch tree bark
- adult helper

**Caution:** *This project involves an open flame and a can of Sterno. The edges of a chisel are sharp. Since this involves use of fire and smoke, do this experiment outdoors in an area that does not get wind or in a well-ventilated room. You'll need an adult helper.*

## Background

Forest fires can devastate thousands of acres (hectares) of valuable woodlands in only a few days. In addition to ruining the natural beauty of wilderness areas, a raging fire can approach homes, businesses, schools, and even consume whole towns if left unchecked. This is why fires have been studied so carefully in recent years—how they start, how they move, and what types of vegetation fuel them. Communities close to natural areas must be particularly cautious about the kinds of trees, bushes, and grasses that surround and encroach upon public areas, since much of this foliage makes excellent combustible fuels for fires. In fact, a sturdy row of white poplars or elms can actually draw a roaring fire down instead of up the side of a hill. Flammable trees, like poplars and elms, are the subject of this project.

## Procedure

Bark samples are cut from trees, each sample having roughly the same 1x2-inch (2.5x5-cm) dimension. One at a time, the samples are placed over a lighted Sterno can and the time it takes for each sample to completely carbonize is noted.

**Hypothesis**

The thicker, more fibrous barks will burn more slowly than the thinner barks.

**Experiment to Test Hypothesis**

**1.** Use the field guide to research areas and find suitable trees. You don't have to cut a sample from all the trees on the list, but make sure you have at least one piece of cedar and one piece of oak.

**2.** With an adult's help, use the hammer and chisel to make two lateral cuts on the bark of each tree about 2 inches (5 cm) long and 1 inch (2.54 cm) apart. Connect the lateral cuts with horizontal cuts at the top and bottom, and carefully peel the square of bark away from the tree.

**3.** Make a small label for each piece of bark and place the label in a corner of each sample.

**4.** Examine each bark sample for color, texture, hardness, and fragrance— making notes when necessary.

**Note:** *To keep the oils in each sample from drying out, proceed with the remaining steps within a 24-hour period.*

**5.** Bend the chicken wire into a U-shape that fits over the can of Sterno. The top surface of the "grill" should be about 3 inches (7.6 cm) from the top of the Sterno can.

**6.** Light the can of Sterno and, using the tongs, place the cedar sample on the grill. Put on an oven mitt and hold the grill above the flame. Time how long it takes for the cedar to completely carbonize. Follow with the remaining bark samples, timing them. When you've burned each sample, close the lid on the can of Sterno to suffocate the flame.

**7.** Compare the various times it took each sample to carbonize, noting significant differences.

**Results & Conclusions**

Of the trees on the list, the fastest burning were the cedar, eucalyptus, and piñon pine, followed by the peppertree. The cedar sample completely carbonized in only 1.2 seconds, followed by the eucalyptus, pine, and peppertree at 2.2, 3.0, and 3.5 seconds, respectively. The sycamore and birch samples burned more slowly, followed by the maple, with the oak sample burning the slowest of all.

Comparing these burn rates contradicted the initial hypothesis that thickness of bark alone would contribute to a bark's flammability, since the thinner birch and sycamore samples burned more slowly than the thicker cedar and pine samples. It was clear that some other factor was more important to burn rates than the thickness of bark.

Looking back over the observations made of each sample before burning yielded the answer. The more fragrant barks—cedar and eucalyptus particularly—burned the fastest. The fragrance of cedar and eucalyptus trees is due to the presence of oils in them—oils which ignite easily and burn quickly. So by far, the most dangerous trees in a forest fire are the ones that smell the best.

# Five

# BUILD *It Better*

# Bottle Altimeter

**Adult Help Required**

*Is it possible to construct a homemade altimeter sensitive enough to measure altitude changes and indicate them on a piece of graph paper?*

## Materials
- large juice bottle with side handles
- 2-foot (60-cm) length clear plastic tubing
- lined index card or graph paper
- rubber cement
- red food coloring
- 1-foot (30-cm) string
- 5x2-inch (12.5x5-cm) strip of cardboard
- ruler
- scissors
- eyedropper
- water
- adult helper

**Caution:** *This project requires using the tip of some scissors to punch a hole in a plastic cup. Since scissors are sharp, have an adult assist you.*

## Background
Scientists know that air has weight, just like water. When we dive into water, we feel pressure on our eardrums from the weight of the water above us. The deeper we dive, the more water is above us and the greater the pressure. In the same way, air at lower altitudes exerts more pressure on our bodies than it does at higher altitudes. Since pressure can be measured by the rising and falling of fluid in a barometer, this same principle can be used to build a slightly more sophisticated instrument that translates pressure readings into an indication of altitude—the altimeter.

## Procedure
An altimeter built from a juice bottle, plastic tubing, and graph paper is tested at various altitudes. The instrument is designed to display measurable changes of altitude by way of a red indicator against graph paper.

## Hypothesis
The instrument will accurately display degrees of changing altitude.

## Experiment to Test Hypothesis
**1.** With an adult's help, make a hole in the center of the plastic juice-bottle cap by twisting the scissors. The hole should be just big enough to contain the plastic tubing.

**2.** Place one end of the tubing through the hole and push it down about 5 inches (12.7 cm). At the place where the tubing goes through the bottle cap, apply some rubber cement to make a seal. You don't want any air leaking into the bottle and spoiling your results.

Bent Plastic
Tubing

**3.** Attach the cap and tubing to the bottle, and carefully bend the tubing into a triangle as shown in the illustration. Be careful not to fold the tubing at the triangle's corners, but just bend it carefully.

**4.** Use the rubber cement to glue a piece of graph paper to the side of the bottle, directly behind the horizontal piece of graph paper. Tape the tubing along the sides of the graph paper.

**5.** Mix red food coloring into just a little water—only 1 or 2 drops are needed.

**6.** Turn the free end of the tubing upward slightly. While holding this end, use the eyedropper to put a few drops of red water into the tube. Put in enough water so that it rolls to the center of the tube and forms a kind of blob. This will be your indicator.

**7.** Using the ruler and scissors, have an adult help you score (make a partial cut) through the center of the cardboard strip so that you can fold it lengthwise.

**8.** Tie the ends of the string around the handles of the bottle, and insert the folded cardboard at the top of the loop for your altimeter handle.

**9.** Lift the altimeter by its handle. This is important because if you touch the bottle, the air will be warmed by your body heat, thereby increasing air pressure, and give you an inaccurate reading.

**10.** Take the altimeter to your basement if you have one, or to the lowest floor of your house. Notice where the indicator blob appears against the graph paper.

**11.** Take the altimeter to the highest level of your house. Measure the difference in graph paper degrees.

**12.** Bring your barometer along on your next elevator ride. Watch what happens.

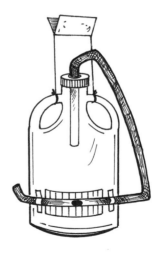

Finished Altimeter

## Results & Conclusions

It appeared that lower altitudes resulted in the indicator blob moving to the right, and higher altitudes moved the blob to the left. Therefore, right-to-left movement meant climbing, while left-to-right movement meant descending. The altimeter meter responded very noticeably to even the smallest variations in altitude. The red indicator blob moved a full 4° on the graph paper when moving the altimeter from the basement to the upper floor. Taking the instrument on an elevator resulted in a 12° difference from ground level to the tenth floor.

From this project, it can be concluded that an altimeter works because of the air pressure differential inside and outside the bottle. When the instrument is in the basement, the air pressure outside the bottle is greater than that inside the bottle. The greater pressure pushes the column of air downward (through the exposed end of tubing), which, in turn, pushes the indicator blob to the right. At a higher altitude, the air pressure inside the bottle is greater, and this pushes the column of air upward (through the enclosed end of tubing), which, in turn, pushes the indicator blob to the left. Both actions equalize the pressure inside and outside of the jar.

# Kitchen Hydrometer

*Is it possible to construct an instrument that detects fluid density from common kitchen materials?*

## Materials
- plastic drinking straw (solid color)
- large paper clip
- ruler
- scissors
- waterproof marking pen
- 2 wide-rim jars (same size)
- measuring cup
- salt
- warm water

## Background
A hydrometer is a simple indicator of fluid density. Sophisticated hydrometers can measure fluid density by identifying the dissolved or suspended particulates in just about any liquid, but it's also possible to construct a simple hydrometer out of basic kitchen materials.

## Procedure
A plastic drinking straw is trimmed, folded, calibrated in millimeters, and weighted with a paper clip to make a usable hydrometer, which is tested in freshwater and saltwater.

*25 millimeters = 1 inch or 2.54 centimeters*

## Hypothesis
The hydrometer will respond differently in the freshwater and saltwater.

## Experiment to Test Hypothesis
**1.** Cut the drinking straw in half with the scissors.

**2.** Use the edge of the ruler to flatten about 2 inches (5 cm) of one end of the straw.

**3.** Fold the flattened end over itself several times and clip the folds together with the large paper clip.

**4.** Measure from the clipped end of the straw and make numbered hatch marks up the length of the straw in millimeters.

**5.** Fill two jars almost to the top with warm water.

**6.** Add 1 cup (240 ml) of salt to one of the jars and stir the water until the salt completely dissolves. Allow the jars to cool.

**7.** Place the hydrometer, paper-clip end down, in the freshwater jar. Observe how much the hydrometer sinks into the water as indicated by the millimeter scale.

**8.** Repeat the previous step using saltwater. Compare the results.

**9.** Add more salt to the saltwater jar and repeat the last step.

## Results & Conclusions

The hypothesis was correct in that the hydrometer did respond differently in the freshwater and saltwater. In the freshwater, the hydrometer sank to the fifth millimeter level—almost to the top of the straw. In saltwater, the hydrometer sank only to the third millimeter level. When more salt was added to the saltwater jar, the hydrometer floated even higher—to about the second millimeter level.

From this project, it can be concluded that it's possible to construct a reliable instrument from everyday materials. The straw hydrometer clearly indicated that the saltwater is denser than the freshwater. This means that saltwater exerts greater pressure and pushes up more strongly—the very same reason a swimmer floats more easily in the ocean than in a freshwater lake.

# A Simple Siphon

*Can water be made to flow between two detached containers until a uniform water level is achieved?*

## Materials
- 2 shallow glasses (same size)
- 1 foot (30 cm) plastic or rubber tubing
- bubble level
- waterproof marking pen or Sharpie
- stack of books
- water

## Background
Even ancient engineers knew it was sometimes necessary to drain water from one container into a second container, hundreds of feet or meters away. The Greek Archimedes was said to have devised an ingenious way of filling wine casks directly from the press, which was located on a hillside hundreds of feet (meters) above the town. Archimedes' simple siphoning method may have saved his servants from climbing the cliffs above Athens with flasks attached to their backs. And for that they were probably very grateful!

*3 feet or 36 inches = 1 yard*

*39 inches = 1 meter*

## Procedure
Two glasses, half-filled with water, are connected by a water-filled tube. One glass is raised above the other, and the flow of water through the tube is observed.

## Hypothesis
The water in the raised glass will completely drain into the lower glass through the tube.

## Experiment to Test Hypothesis
1. Fill both glasses half-full with water.

2. Insert one end of the tubing into the first glass. Gently suck on the opposite end of the tubing until water completely fills the tubing.

3. Remove the tubing from your mouth and quickly place a finger over the end to stop the water from flowing out.

4. With your finger still in place, place the stopped end of the tubing into the second glass. Remove your finger.

5. Place the first glass on top of a stack of books. Watch the water level changing in each glass and mark it.

**6.** Put the edge of the level against the marks you made on the glasses and check the bubble for straightness.

**7.** Place the second glass on the stack of books and watch the water levels again. Mark them and check for straightness with the level.

## Results & Conclusions

The hypothesis was incorrect in that the water did not completely empty from the higher glass into the lower one. Instead, water from the higher glass moved through the tube into the lower glass, but stopped at a certain point. When no more water appeared to be flowing between the two glasses, the water level on each glass was marked. The level revealed that the "waterline" was even across the two glasses!

By sucking water through the tubing to create a vacuum, water was free to flow through the tubing without any interference from the air. When one side of the tubing is lower than the other, the weight of the water in the lower part is greater than the weight in the upper part. Since water molecules "stick together," the length of tubing that contains the greater weight of water draws the remaining water behind it. This continues until the water levels are the same for both glasses. From this we can conclude that when water levels between the two glasses equalize, the siphoning action stops.

# Smelt Bismuth at Home

*Can a usable bismuth disk be created by smelting and refining the crude bismuth found in bird shot?*

## Materials
- aluminum soda-pop can
- oven mitt
- metal tablespoon (discard after using)
- bismuth bird shot (available in sporting goods stores)
- vegetable cooking oil
- safety pin
- fine-grade sandpaper
- masking tape
- stovetop burner
- adult helper

**Caution:** *It's important to work closely with an adult for every step of this project.*

## Background
The behavior of the metal bismuth in a magnetic field is important in our understanding of magnetism. Bismuth displays important diamagnetic properties when exposed to either pole of the magnetic field—that is, it will always repulse the field—and so is the most widely used substance for experiments with diamagnetism.

Bismuth is soft, heavy, brittle, and silvery pink in color. Unlike most materials, it expands by 3.32% on solidification, a property it shares with water, gallium, germanium, and antimony. This is useful in casting alloys where adding a little bismuth keeps the alloy from shrinking away from the mold or forming shrinkage cracks. Because bismuth expands when cooled, solid bismuth—filled with crystals—is less dense than molten bismuth.

Unlike most heavy metals, bismuth is recognized as one of the environmentally safest elements, and is noncarcinogenic. A growing number of industrial applications use bismuth as a substitute for more toxic metals like lead. Bismuth is easy to melt and cools relatively quickly. Because lead is toxic and bismuth is safe (it's the active ingredient in Pepto-Bismol stomach medicine), it can be found in sporting goods stores in the form of environmentally safe bird shot. Bismuth is also used in some fishing lures as a replacement for lead.

This project will melt a small quantity of bismuth shot to make a solid disk of bismuth. In disk form, the bismuth will demonstrate interesting diamagnetic properties and is a necessary component in other magnetic experiments.

## Procedure

We melt 1 tablespoon (15 ml) of bismuth shot over an open burner to remove impurities. The molten bismuth is then poured into a mold made from an aluminum soda-pop can.

## Hypothesis

After cooling, the bismuth disk will be removed from the mold, sanded and polished, and provide a useful component for the Strange Levitating Magnet project.

## Experiment to Test Hypothesis

**1.** Turn an empty aluminum soda-pop can upside down and tape the base securely to a flat surface. The dimple in the bottom of the can will be the mold for the molten bismuth. Make sure the can is no more than 1 foot (30 cm) from the burner where you'll be heating the bismuth.

**2.** Dip a disposable tablespoon in cooking oil and shake off the excess oil. Then fill the tablespoon ¾ full (11.25 ml) with bismuth shot. With an adult's help, heat the spoon over a stove until the shot begins to melt into a solid mass. Use an oven mitt to hold the spoon.

**3.** As the bismuth continues to melt, the cooking oil will float to the surface and protect the bismuth from oxygen, which can form black oxides at the surface of the bismuth. If oxides form, open the safety pin and use the pin end to scrape the oxides to the side of the spoon.

**Caution:** *Hot cooking oil can sputter and burn you, as can melting bismuth.*

**4.** *Very carefully* move the spoon over to the upside-down aluminum can, and pour the metal into the hollow dimple.

**5.** Allow the bismuth to cool overnight. Test the cooling the next day by touching the aluminum can. If sufficiently cooled, hold the mold under warm running water until the bismuth disk pops out. Use fine sandpaper to polish both sides of the disk.

## Results & Conclusions

It was very important to have two people—one an adult—working together closely on this project. The shot melted easily in the spoon, and the cooking oil kept most of the oxides from forming. The few tissuelike oxides that did form were easily scraped to the side of the spoon with the safety pin. The bismuth was poured into the mold from the side of the spoon opposite the collected oxides.

The aluminum can, after cooling overnight, was touched and found to be at room temperature. The bismuth disk popped out of the mold easily after running the mold through warm water for about one minute. At first, the shape of the disk seemed problematical since it was flat on one side but curved like a convex lens on the other. But sanding the curved side flattened it to the point where wobble was removed and the disk could sit securely on a flat surface.

# Strange Levitating Magnet

*Adult Help Required*

*Is it possible to levitate a neodymium pellet between a stack of permanent magnets and a bismuth disk?*

---

## Materials

- 5x5x¾-inch (12.5x12.5 x 1.8-cm) piece of plywood
- 2x¾x12½-inch (5x1.8 x 31.25-cm) piece of wood (not plywood)
- ¾₆-inchx1 foot (5-mmx30 cm) threaded rod
- five ¾₆-inch (5-mm) hexagonal nuts
- two ¾₆-inch (5-mm) washers
- 1½-inch (3.8-cm) bismuth disk
- neodymium magnetic pellet
- fifteen 1⅛-inch (2.8-cm) ring magnets
- nails
- epoxy glue
- pencil
- ruler
- drill
- ¾₆-inch (or 5-mm) drill bit
- hammer
- screwdriver
- small saw
- adult helper

**Caution:** *Ask an adult to assist you in cutting and drilling the wood pieces.*

**Note:** *If ¾₆-inch drill bits, hexagonal nuts, washers, and threaded rods are not available in your country, use 5-mm bit, washers, hexagonal nuts, and a threaded rod.*

*We've rounded up to 5 mm, a typical size for precision tools.*

*¾₆ inches = 0.47 cm or 4.7 mm*

*Bismuth disks and neodymium magnetic pellets are available from numerous online science supply stores. Or, you can make your own bismuth disks from environmentally safe bird shot. See the project "Smelt Bismuth at Home," pp. 105–106.*

## Background

Magnetism reveals many things about the behavior of atomic particles that make up all matter. When materials, such as silver, gold, bismuth, water, and even living tissue, are placed in a strong magnetic field, their billions of electrons change positions to resist the magnet's influence. Disturbed electrons shift their orbits to create their own magnetic field, and as a result, the atoms in a material like bismuth behave as little magnetic needles pointing in the direction opposite to the applied field.

This is the principle of diamagnetism. When exposed to *either pole* of a magnet, diamagnetic materials are repulsed and move away from it. With an extremely powerful electromagnet, it's even possible to diamagnetically levitate a living creature due to the water, protein, and DNA in its body. A drop of water could be levitated with a strong enough magnetic field. This has been done with large electromagnets, but not yet with permanent magnets.

Some materials show stronger diamagnetic properties than others. The heavy metal bismuth is used for this project because it's about 20 times more diamagnetic than water. Using bismuth, a neodymium (rare-earth) magnet, and a stack of ring magnets, magnetic levitation can be created and sustained in a simple model.

## Procedure

Within a simple wooden framework, a neodymium pellet is placed between an adjustable stack of ring magnets and a fixed bismuth disk.

## Hypothesis

By fine-tuning the model, the pellet should float several millimeters above the bismuth.

> *1 millimeter = 0.039 inch*
> *1 centimeter = 0.039 inch*

## Experiment to Test Hypothesis

**1.** Cut the 12½-inch (31.25 cm) piece of wood into two parts, one that's 8¾ inches (22 cm) long and another that's 3¾ inches (9.25 cm) long. Drill a hole with the ³⁄₁₆-inch (or 5-mm) bit in the center of the smaller part.

**2.** Make an L-shape by nailing the larger part into the smaller part. Turn the L upside down and nail it near the back edge of the plywood square,

centering it. The short part of the L should hang over the square.

**3.** Insert the threaded rod through the hole and push it down until it touches the plywood. Lift the rod up slightly and slide the bismuth disk underneath the rod, centering it. Trace around the disk with a pencil; then remove the rod and disk.

**4.** Using the trace mark you made, glue the bismuth disk to the plywood. Allow the glue to dry overnight.

**5.** Reinsert the rod and place two nuts at the top end. Screw the nuts down about 5 inches (12.7 cm) so that the rod hangs from the L, secured by the nuts.

**6.** Place a washer and nut at the bottom end of the rod, and screw the washer along the rod until it's snug against the wood. Follow with a nut and washer (note the reverse order) and screw the nut along the rod to about the halfway point.

**7.** Starting from the bottom of the rod, stack the 15 ring magnets and screw a final washer and nut to the bottom tip of the rod to secure the stack. Tighten the nuts on both sides of the stack.

**8.** Twist the threaded rod so that the stack is about 3 inches (7.6 cm) from the bismuth disk. Place the neodymium pellet in the center of the disk and slowly twist the rod so that the magnet stack moves closer to the pellet. Observe the pellet carefully.

## Results & Conclusions

The first few tries at moving the magnet stack closer to the neodymium pellet resulted in the pellet springing up and sticking to the bottom-most magnet of the stack. This was corrected by twisting the shaft very slowly and watching for movement in the pellet. When the pellet shifted, we slowed the twisting even further and gently blew on the pellet.

Surprisingly, it began to spin, due to the fact that it was making only minimum contact with the bismuth—or half-floating! A few more slow twists and the levitation became more pronounced. The pellet could now be seen gently bobbing in midair about 2 millimeters above the bismuth disk.

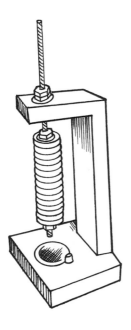

Here was an object captured in a fascinating flux of magnetic forces—a kind of magnetic and gravitational balancing act. Above, the stack of ring magnets attracted the neodymium pellet with just enough force to keep it from falling. Below, the diamagnetic bismuth repulsed the pellet with just enough force to keep it buoyed. So the pellet floated in a weightless zone where gravity was neutralized by both attractive and repulsive magnetic forces.

The pellet was horizontally stable, since the ring magnets created a magnetic field in a shape that kept the pellet centered and prevented it from flying out to the side. But the pellet was vertically unstable, and could easily, with a nudge, fly up and stick to the magnets again. This was corrected below by the diamagnetic interaction between the bismuth and the pellet. Here a complementary magnetic field was created in a shape that stabilized the pellet vertically. The result was a levitated, stable neodymium pellet spinning in thin air—a true marvel!

# Sun-Warmed Balloon

*Can the cool air in a sealed garbage bag be heated sufficiently by the sun to turn the bag into a hot-air balloon?*

## Materials
- black plastic garbage bag (lightweight, not heavy-duty)
- twist-tie
- about 60 inches (150 cm) kite string
- air conditioner
- brick

## Background
For over 200 years, the science of hot-air ballooning has been developed, perfected, and put to good use. Once mostly a fantasy in Jules Verne novels, travel by balloon became practical with the discovery of lighter-than-air gases, such as hydrogen and helium. The need for faster and more controllable methods of air transportation has made ballooning an activity mainly for hobbyists these days. Still, a balloon that rises on hot air alone is a marvel to see—if it can be made to happen.

## Procedure
A lightweight black plastic garbage bag is filled with cold air, sealed, and tethered to a brick in full sunlight. The bag is observed throughout the day to see if it rises.

## Hypothesis
After several hours in direct sunlight, the garbage bag will rise off the ground, but only a few inches (say, 7 to 10 cm).

## Experiment to Test Hypothesis
**1.** If you have access to a window-mounted air-conditioning unit, shake open the bag and fill it with cold blowing air. Otherwise, find the coolest spot in an air-conditioned supermarket or restaurant.

**2.** Close the bag and twist it until the bag is balloonlike. Place a twist-tie around the bag to seal it, and trim away any excess bag (the part you twisted closed) with the scissors.

**3.** Take the bag outside to a sunny spot that will remain sunny throughout most of the day. Tie the twisted end of the bag to the brick with about 5 feet (150 cm) of kite string.

**4.** Allow the bag to sit in the sun, checking it at one-hour intervals.

**Results & Conclusions**

Our bag, filled with air-conditioned air, was placed on an asphalt driveway where it sat on its side. Since the day was already heating up by the time of placement (11:00 A.M.), it didn't take long before the bag turned upright and appeared to move closer to the brick. By noon the bag was "standing up" right next to the brick, although it was still very much touching the ground.

The real excitement started around 3:00 P.M., when a small length of tether could be seen trailing underneath the balloon, which had risen a few inches (cm) off the ground. By four o'clock the rise was clearly noticeable—a full foot (30 cm)—and by five-thirty, the balloon had risen to about 14 inches (36 cm) above the ground. True to our hypothesis, the balloon rose, but more than the few inches (cm) predicted. Maybe a longer (or hotter) day would have resulted in seeing the balloon rise the length of its tether and even strain against it.

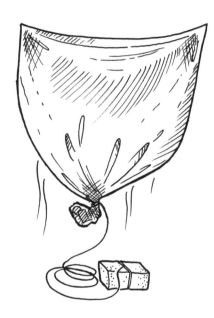

# Triangles & Bridges

*Why are triangles important in the design of a bridge?*

## Materials
- camera
- highlighter pen
- fourteen 6x1 inch (15x2.54cm) strips of cardboard
- two 6½x12 inch spans of cardboard
- 14 brass fasteners
- sharp pencil
- 2 paper cups
- pennies or similar coins
- 4 stacks of books
- glue

## Background
Bridges are some of the oldest architectural structures and were designed to allow people and cargo to pass across water, ravines, or difficult terrain. A well-engineered bridge is designed to support weight without collapsing or deforming. There are three types of weight, or loads, that the engineer must consider when designing a bridge. The first, called the *dead load*, is mainly the weight of the bridge itself. The second load is the changing weight of the people or vehicles that pass across the bridge. The third load consists of forces of nature such as wind, rain, or ice. Sometimes engineers combine the second and third loads into the *design load*.

The distance a bridge extends between two supports is called a *span*. There are two basic stresses that act on a span: compression and tension. If you place a plank of wood between two supports and put some weight on it, the wood will bend slightly. The top surface of the wood pushes together from the weight, while the bottom surface pulls apart. These two types of stresses—*compressive* for the pushing together and *tensile* for the pulling apart—will eventually cause the unsupported plank to break in half. This is why bridge engineers experimented with different types of triangular supports, or trestles, for their plank bridges.

## Procedure
We photograph actual bridges to document the use of triangles in trestle designs. We build a square and triangular trestle and test each for tensile strength. Finally we create square and triangular trestles to support model bridges, each of which is weighed and compared for strength.

## Hypothesis
The triangular trestle will prove to be the strongest support for a plank bridge.

## Experiment to Test Hypothesis

**I.** Observe some bridges in your area. Take a camera to photograph them. Bridge designs you see might include the Pratt, Warren, K-Design, or Baltimore.

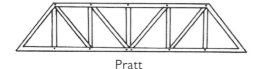
Pratt

Warren

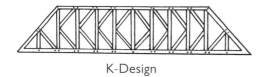
K-Design

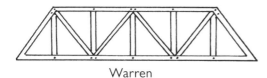
Baltimore

Use a highlighter pen over your developed photos to trace a few triangles you see in each of the bridge designs.

**2.** Arrange three cardboard strips into two triangles and punch holes in the corners using the sharp pencil. Place a fastener in each hole. Arrange the remaining eight strips into squares. Take one of the squares and twist it. You can see that it easily deforms into another shape. Now try twisting a triangle. The triangle holds its shape and will not distort under pressure.

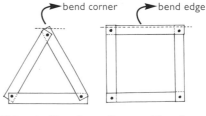
Triangle Trestle    Square Trestle

**3.** Fold the top corner of each triangle and the top edge of each square. Attach a bead of glue to the folded parts and place triangles and squares side by side between two stacks of books. Carefully lay a cardboard span across each pair of triangles and squares, spanning the books, so that you have two bridges—one with triangular trestles and one with square trestles.

**4.** Place a paper cup on the square bridge. Add pennies to the cup, keeping count. Count the number of pennies it takes to make the bridge sag or even collapse. Repeat this process for the triangle bridge. Compare the amount of pennies it took to make each bridge collapse.

## Results & Conclusions

When we fastened the strips into squares and triangles, we could easily see that the triangle held its shape under stress while the square could be deformed. This principle was further demonstrated by using the squares and triangles as trestles for our bridges. The bridge supported by triangles was able to hold more penny weight than the bridge supported by squares, confirming our hypothesis that triangles are essential structural elements in bridge design.

# Water Clock

*Is it possible, following an ancient design, to construct a water clock that accurately tells the time?*

## Materials
- large widemouthed jar (mayonnaise jar)
- small, narrow jar (capers or olives jar)
- old cotton T-shirt
- marking pen
- food coloring
- rubber cement
- aluminum foil
- cellophane tape
- scissors
- clock
- water

## Background
For thousands of years, people have been using water to tell time. A 12th century manuscript recently found in an English monastery mentions a fire that burned several structures before it could be extinguished by water carried from the *magnus horologium*—Latin for "big clock"!

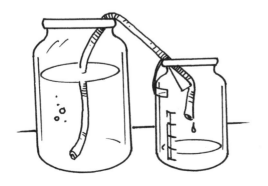

Dripping water is what scientists call a quantum process. The "beats" of the dripping water occur at fairly regular intervals and even resemble the ticks of a mechanical clock. In this way, time is measured in regular pulses and the accumulation of water indicates the passage of hours. The simplest way to do this is through a simple siphon device, described in Chapter 5. However, we'll use a water wick made of cotton cloth for a more clocklike effect.

## Procedure
A water wick, made from a piece of cotton T-shirt, connects two glasses. The wick draws water from one glass and drips it into a second glass, which is marked with every hour.

## Hypothesis
The water clock will prove to be an accurate time-measuring device.

## Experiment to Test Hypothesis
**1.** Use the scissors to cut a rectangular strip from the T-shirt, 12x2 inches (30x3 cm). Add a small string of rubber cement to one long edge and roll the strip from the opposite edge into a tight cylinder.

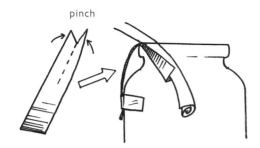

pinch

Gutter Detail

**2.** Remove labels from the jars so that you can see through them clearly. Fill the wide jar with water and add some food coloring.

**3.** Fold some aluminum foil into a narrow strip about 4x½ inches (10x1.25 cm) long, and tape it to the side of the narrow jar as shown in the illustration. Make a "gutter" by pinching lengthwise the part of the strip inside the jar.

**4.** Put one end of the wick into the wide jar, bend it over the edge, and place the other end of the wick into the aluminum foil gutter of the narrow jar. The wick should not touch the rim of the narrow jar.

**5.** Wait for the wick to fill with water and for the first drop to appear at the end placed in the narrow jar. When the drop falls, note the time.

**6.** After a half hour passes, notice the water level in the narrow jar and make a mark on the outside of the jar. Do this again after another half hour so that you have two half-hour markings.

**7.** Continue marking the jar every half hour until the narrow jar is filled to the top. You can then determine how many "hours" of water the jar contains.

**Results & Conclusions**
After placing the wick in the bottles, it took several minutes for it to fill with water and begin dripping from the lower end. Once started, however, the dripping was steady and regular. The size and thickness of this particular wick, along with the dimensions of the narrow jar, allowed for the accumulation of about ¾ inch (1.9 cm) of water every hour. This could obviously be adjusted by changing either wick or jar size.

A water clock operates by two processes: siphoning and capillary action. With capillary action, water molecules are attracted more to a narrow gap between solids than to a wider one. This means that water is actually drawn up through the threads of the cotton until it reaches the bend over the jar's rim. At this point, siphoning aids capillary action because—since water is also attracted to itself—the weight of water going down the wick pulls water after it. This gentle pull of water terminates at the wick's end, where the water accumulates into a droplet which soon becomes heavy enough to break away from the cotton and fall into the jar, creating one "tick" of the clock!

# Watt's Micrometer

*Is it possible to construct a micrometer, after an 18th century design, that provides reliable and accurate measurements?*

## Materials
- 3x6 inches (about 7.5x15 cm) plywood
- 7-inch (17.8-cm) long bolt and six-sided nut to fit
- coping saw
- small metal square (offcut or scrap)
- protractor
- ruler
- pencil
- 10 colors of acrylic paint
- fine paintbrush
- vise
- epoxy adhesive
- adult helper

**Caution:** *A coping saw can be a dangerous tool. Make sure an adult assists you for the steps that require cutting.*

**Note:** *For accurate measuring, the bolt should be ¾-inch UNC-style (or about 18 to 20 mm), available in good hardware stores.*

## Background
In the late 18th century, the British inventor James Watt created a new measuring instrument from a horseshoe and threaded shaft. His *micrometer* soon provided engineers with measurements so precise that the device revolutionized the design and construction of huge steam engines and other mechanical marvels of the day. Micrometers are still used to measure the thickness of parts, diameters of shafts, and depths of slots. The precision of a micrometer—measurements to the order of 0.001 inch—is achieved through the mechanics of a calibrated screw mechanism.

An engineer's micrometer can be a very expensive item, but the following project constructs an accurate one from easy-to-find materials.

## Procedure
Plywood, metal, and a UNC-style bolt are combined to create a usable and accurate micrometer.

## Hypothesis
The homemade micrometer will accurately measure the width of coins (such as two U.S. quarters) and the measurement should be the same for each.

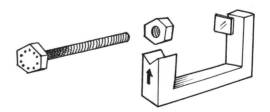

## Experiment to Test Hypothesis

**1.** Use the coping saw to cut out the middle of the 3x6-inch (7.6x15.24-cm) rectangle, leaving a strip ½ inch (1.25 cm) wide along the long side, ½ inch (1.25 cm) at one end, and 1 inch (2.54 cm) at the other end. Saw 1 inch (2.54 cm) off the thicker strip, turning the rectangle into a wide U-shape with a long, narrow strip and a short, wider strip.

**2.** Fasten the U-shape in a vise and use the protractor to mark a 120° angle just below the top of the wider strip. Carefully saw away the wood to make a V-shaped groove that fits the edges of a six-sided nut.

**3.** Squeeze some epoxy adhesive into the groove and insert the nut. After the glue hardens (overnight), screw the 7-inch (17.8-cm) bolt into the nut so that the bolt touches the other side of the rectangle. Mark this contact point in pencil, and glue the metal square to the frame at this point. Make sure that the surface of the metal is exactly at right angles to the length of the bolt.

**4.** With the protractor guiding you, paint ten different colored dots at 36-degree intervals around the bolt head. The dots will allow you to measure something to the accuracy of a hundredth of an inch (0.254 mm). Right below the bolt head on the edge of the wide strip, paint a guide line so that you can keep track of how many times you twist the bolt while measuring.

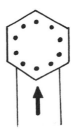

*1/100 inch = 0.254 millimeters or 0.0254 centimeters*

*1/50 inch = 0.508 millimeters or 0.0508 centimeters*

*1/10 inch = 2.54 millimeters or 0.254 centimeters*

**5.** To use the micrometer, screw in the bolt until it touches the metal square. Measure the quarter (or any object) on the conventional ruler first. Since ten revolutions of the UNC bolt equals 1 inch (2.54 cm) of length, and the quarter is about 1 inch (2.54 cm) wide, unscrew the bolt 15 revolutions (1½ inches or 3.8 cm) so that you can place the quarter between the end of the bolt and the metal plate. Note the color of the "home dot," the dot directly above the guide line.

**6.** Hold the quarter between the metal plate and bolt head, and slowly twist the bolt until it makes contact with the edge of the quarter. Keep track of how far the home dot rotates from the guide line before the bolt touches the quarter. (Remember that one complete rotation represents one tenth of an inch and fractions of rotations represent hundredths of an inch.)

**7.** Deduct the twisting measurement from the measurement you started with—namely, 1½ inches (3.8 cm)—to find a very precise measurement for the quarter.

## Results & Conclusions

Our micrometer provided a measurement which was shorter than the conventional ruler measurement by "two dots," or one-fiftieth of an inch.

Surprisingly, the second quarter we measured deviated by one-hundredth of an inch. This reflects either some imprecision in our instrument or actual minute variations in the sizes of quarters. Measuring the same two quarters a second time yielded identical results, and a third quarter we measured surprised us with a width of exactly one inch. From this, we conclude that all quarters are not created equal!

# Six

# CREATIVE
# *Chemistry*

# Colorful Candy

*How many color dyes are used in a piece of candy?*

## Materials
- blotting paper
- packet of Smarties (Use a red or purple one.)
- plate
- water
- cotton swab (Q-tip)

## Background

Food manufacturers use many complicated chemical processes to make foods attractive and delicious. Candy companies are especially enthusiastic about creating candies in new shapes, colors, and flavors. This means that even the simplest-looking candy may contain many chemical surprises when you break it apart or dissolve it in water.

Water-based dyes can be isolated from certain candies by the process of *chromatography*. The different dyes that combine to make candy color can be separated through blotting paper. This is because when you wet the candy, the water containing the dyes is drawn through the paper by *capillary action*, a process whereby water molecules are attracted more to a narrow gap between solids than to a wider one. Through capillary action, water is drawn up through the fibers of the blotting paper, pulling the molecules of dye with it.

The larger dye molecules stay close to the candy, while the smaller molecules bleed out farther from the candy. In this way, you can see which colors of dye have the smaller molecules.

## Procedure

A purple or red Smartie will be placed on blotting paper. The candy will be moistened with a little water so that the dyes are drawn through the paper.

## Hypothesis

A ring of different colors will radiate out from the moistened Smartie, even though the candy is only one color.

## Experiment to Test Hypothesis

**1.** Cut the blotting paper into a circle, 6 inches (15.24 cm) in diameter.

**2.** Place the circle of blotting paper on the plate.

**3.** Put the Smartie in the center of the blotting paper.

**4.** Wet the cotton swab and quickly touch it against the candy so that a drop of water coats the candy surface. After a few seconds, repeat this until a circle of water moves out from the candy.

**5.** Leave the wet Smartie alone for about 15 minutes; then record your observations.

## Results & Conclusions

Our hypothesis was correct in that rings of different colors of dyes were drawn out from the Smartie, but dramatic results took a full day of soaking the candy and allowing it to slowly dissolve on the blotting paper.

Our purple Smartie left a ring of pink—a color nearly completely invisible in the dry candy—that blended into a wider ring of purple fringed with blue. The red Smartie produced a corona of pink fading to orange fading to yellow. It was a surprise to see which colors stayed close to the candy and which were drawn away from the candy. This meant that dye molecules of certain colors, such as blues and yellows, are smaller than those that comprise reds and purples. The results of the project made it clear that what appears as a single color in a candy is actually a combination of many colors of dyes.

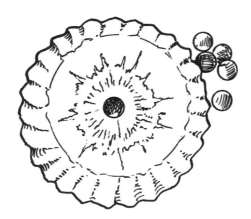

# Compare Soft-Drink Densities

*When placed in a tank of water, will the soft-drink cans sink or float, and what does their behavior tell us about fluid density?*

## Materials

- aluminum can of regular cola
- aluminum can of diet cola
- aluminum can of uncarbonated fruit juice
- empty fish aquarium (or similar large transparent container)
- masking tape
- waterproof marking pen

**Note:** *It's important to use a clear, filtered fruit juice and not a fruit nectar that may contain pulp.*

## Background

Since a denser liquid will push up more strongly on an object, causing it to float more easily (see "Kitchen Hydrometer," p. 101), it can be assumed that a dense liquid will sink more easily when suspended in a less dense liquid. All the soft drinks used in this project have different amounts of sugars, colorings, and other additives. Therefore, each should reveal a different density, which will be illustrated by how easily each can floats in water.

## Procedure

In changing pairs, the cans of cola, diet cola, and fruit juice are placed in the tank of water and their ability to float is compared.

## Hypothesis

The regular cola and fruit juice will sink to the bottom while the diet cola will float.

## Experiment to Test Hypothesis

**1.** Put masking tape around each can and use a marking pen to label each as diet cola, regular cola, or fruit juice. Using the can labels alone can be confusing to viewers.

**2.** Carefully place the diet cola and regular cola in the water and observe the results.

**3.** Remove the diet cola and leave the regular cola in the water.

**4.** Carefully place the can of fruit juice in the water. Watch what happens.

**5.** As a finale, put the diet cola back into the water and compare all three cans. Observe and compare.

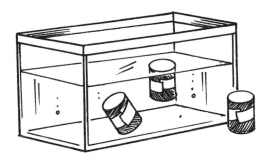

## Results & Conclusions

Although basically correct, our hypothesis had a surprising twist. It was true that the can of regular cola sank nearly to the bottom while the can of diet cola sank just to the top lid. But when the diet cola was removed and the can of fruit juice added, the juice sank all the way to the bottom (bouncing off the bottom, in fact!) while the regular cola continued to bob lightly. Placing the diet cola back in the water gave the clearest comparison of soft-drink densities, with diet cola the least dense, followed by regular cola, followed by the fruit juice.

Comparing the labels of the soft drinks provided a clue. The diet cola was the least dense because, expectedly, it contained no sugar at all but a considerably lighter sugar additive. The regular cola contained both sugar and high-fructose corn syrup—both ingredients adding to the density of the cola. The fruit juice contained corn syrup only, which was initially puzzling because something was still making the juice the heaviest of all.

The answer came in reading the cola label again. Cola and other "fizzy" drinks are made from carbonated water. To carbonate a soft drink, food chemists add carbon-dioxide gas. This light gas, which escapes in the form of bubbles when you open the can, displaces some of the liquid and makes it less dense. This means that a carbonated drink will always have the tendency to be less dense than a filtered, uncarbonated juice drink.

# Hidden Colors in Green

*Why do green trees change their color in the fall?*

**Adult Help Required**

## Materials
- blotting paper or superabsorbent paper towel
- green leaves from deciduous trees, like elm, maple, or oak
- cooking pot
- small Pyrex bowl
- isopropyl alcohol (rubbing alcohol)
- teaspoon
- pencil
- heat source
- adult helper

**Caution:** *This project uses alcohol over a heat source. Alcohol is highly flammable and should not be exposed to an open flame. Make sure an adult helps with the pigment extraction part of this project.*

## Background
In cool climates, everyone enjoys the spectacle of the leaves "turning color." Almost overnight, groves of uniformly green trees turn brilliant hues of yellow, orange, purple, and red. This change results from chemical processes that take place in the trees as the season changes from summer to winter.

Botanists, the scientists who study plants, have identified four pigments in the plant world: *chlorophylls* (green), *carotenoids* (yellow and orange), *tannins* (brown), and *anthocyanins* (pink and purple). These pigments can be most clearly seen in brightly colored flowers, but they also exist—all four of them!—in green leaves.

Of the four, the chlorophylls are key to understanding the changing colors of fall. Green chlorophyll is a key ingredient during the spring and summer months when trees use the energy of the sun to combine carbon dioxide and water into sugars. During a tree's growing season, chlorophyll is produced in great quantities, so that its green pigment masks all the other pigments in the leaves. But as the days get shorter and temperatures drop, the leaves stop their food-making process, and chlorophyll production ceases. The green color of the leaves fades and other pigments in the leaf can then reveal themselves.

## Procedure
An assortment of leaves from deciduous trees is crushed and boiled in alcohol to release the pigments. Blotting paper is suspended over the alcohol to draw up various hues in a chromatograph.

## Hypothesis

The green pigment, extracted from the leaves and dissolved in alcohol, will reveal "fall colors" as it passes up through the blotting paper.

## Experiment to Test Hypothesis

**1.** Shred the leaf samples and place them in the Pyrex bowl. Use the back of a teaspoon (or small spoon) to crush the shreds into a mash.

**2.** Add just enough rubbing alcohol to the bowl to cover the mash.

**3.** Place the bowl in the cooking pot and pour enough water into the pot to surround the bowl.

**4.** With an adult's help, heat the pot until the alcohol in the bowl boils. Allow for adequate ventilation since the fumes of alcohol can be unpleasant.

**5.** Observe the mash of leaves and remove the pot from the heat when the leaves lose their color and the alcohol turns green. Allow the pot and bowl to cool for at least a half hour before continuing. When adequately cool, remove the bowl from the pot.

**6.** Cut a strip from the blotting paper long enough to reach the bottom of the bowl. Use the pencil to make a hole in the paper near the top.

**7.** With the pencil inserted through the paper, suspend the paper over the bowl so that the end of the paper dips into the alcohol. Watch what happens.

## Results & Conclusions

Almost immediately, the alcohol was drawn up through the blotting paper, dragging the green pigment with it. However, as the pigment continued to climb through the paper, the green color began to fade and another color—red— took its place. The red ascended for a while, only to be replaced by orange and then yellow—all colors that were completely invisible in the green-leaf samples.

This *chromatograph* revealed, as stated in our hypothesis, the various fall colors hidden in the ordinary green of leaves. A chromatograph works through capillary action, a process whereby the molecules in a liquid are attracted to smaller gaps in a porous material than to larger ones. Through capillary action, alcohol was drawn up through the fibers of the blotting paper, pulling the particles of dye with it. The larger dye particles (greens and reds) stuck close to the bottom of the strip, while the smaller particles (yellows) bled out farther. In this way, it was possible to see which pigments had the smaller molecules.

# Juice Dehydration

*What will happen if we add a dehydrating agent like polymer crystals to orange juice?*

---

## Materials
- 1 cup orange juice
- resealable plastic bag
- superabsorbent polymer crystals (cross-linked polyacrylamide copolymer flakes, available in science supply stores)
- tablespoon
- bowl
- adult helper

**Caution:** *Do not discard polymer crystal material down the sink, garbage disposal, or toilet. The swelling action of the crystals can damage plumbing. Discard in the trash can only.*

## Background
Juice, soda, milk, and other potable liquids are mostly water with flavorings in the form of sugar, pulp, or fat. Polymer crystals are useful to scientists because they can absorb up to 300 times their weight in water. In fact, polymer crystals absorb only water, which makes them useful in many ways. Water, absorbed in a crystal, does not evaporate as easily, and so the crystals can be added to soil to reduce the amount of water required to keep plants healthy.

The crystals have also been added to clothing, such as shirts or shorts used when exercising, to keep perspiration away from the body. In this project, the crystals will absorb the water in the orange juice so that we can examine what's left behind.

## Procedure
A cup of orange juice is placed in a resealable plastic bag and 1 tablespoon (15 ml) of polymer crystals is added. The juice is mixed with the crystals by kneading the bag, and the bag left overnight.

## Hypothesis
The crystals will absorb the water and orange pulp will be left behind.

## Experiment to Test Hypothesis

**1.** Pour 1 cup (240 ml) of orange juice into the resealable bag.

**2.** Add 1 tablespoon (15 ml) of polymer crystals.

**3.** Seal the bag and knead the juice and crystals for about 2 minutes.

**4.** Place the bag where it won't be disturbed and leave it overnight.

**5.** Carefully unseal the bag, pour the contents in a bowl, and observe the results.

## Results & Conclusions

After leaving the bag undisturbed overnight, the juice and crystals became a mass of orange slime resembling crumbly Jell-O. Upon closer examination, it appeared that the material was composed of jellylike chunks, swollen with water, but coated with a layer of orange pulp and sugar. Since the volume of water-containing chunks was far greater than the volume of pulp and sugar coating, it was clear that the orange juice was mostly water.

# Make a Polymer Jelly

*Is it possible to connect simple polyvinyl acetate molecules in glue into larger polymers?*

## Materials
- borax (cleansing agent or water softener available in hardware stores)
- white liquid glue (or 4% solution of polyvinyl alcohol)
- water
- food coloring
- resealable plastic bag
- measuring cup

**Note:** *For a less rubbery and more transparent jelly that shows off the color better, substitute in equal portions a 4% solution of polyvinyl alcohol instead of white glue. Most science supply stores carry it.*

## Background
White glue, varnishes, and some paints contain a form of liquid plastic made from polyvinyl acetate molecules. The small size of these molecules allows the plastic to remain in a liquid form so that it can be spread evenly over surfaces.

However, certain mineral substances such as borax (made from sodium, boron, oxygen, and water) can connect small polyvinyl acetate molecules into larger chains called polymers. Adding borax transforms plastic in a liquid state to something more like jelly or slime. Polymer substances are flexible, not hard or breakable. Some everyday polymers include Styrofoam and chewing gum.

## Procedure
Glue, water, and borax are combined to make a polymer substance.

## Hypothesis
The liquid glue will become jellylike after adding the water and borax solution.

## Experiment to Test Hypothesis
**1.** Add 1½ teaspoons (7.5 ml) of borax to ½ cup (120 ml) of water and stir until the borax dissolves.

**2.** Add food coloring to this solution until you have a deep color.

**3.** Mix ¼ cup (60 ml) of glue with an equal amount of water.

**4.** In a resealable plastic bag, add the borax solution to the glue solution. Knead the bag until you feel the solutions thickening.

**5.** Remove the polymer substance and examine it.

**6.** Store your jelly in a plastic bag, and keep it in the refrigerator for future use.

**7.** Since borax can irritate the eyes, always wash your hands after playing with your jelly.

**Results & Conclusions**

After mixing the solutions in the plastic bag and kneading them together, it became apparent to us that the material was thickening. In about two minutes, the material had a uniform jellylike consistency that fell out of the bag in a "chunk" but soon melted into a pool. Playing with the jelly showed that you could mold it into shapes, but that the shapes dissolved after a few minutes. It was clear that the borax was a "cross-linking agent," chemically altering the molecular structure of the glue so that the smaller polyvinyl acetate molecules combined to form larger polymers.

# Measure Sugar in Soft Drinks

*How many teaspoons of sugar are in a 12-fluid-ounce (360-ml) can of soft drink?*

## Materials
- calibrated hydrometer
- 12-fluid-ounce (360-ml) can of cola or similar soft drink
- 2 large water glasses (same size)
- measuring cup
- teaspoon
- water
- sugar

**Note:** *For a calibrated kitchen hydrometer, see page 101.*

> *1 teaspoon = 5 milliliters*
> *1 cup = 8 fluid ounces = 240 milliliters*

## Background
All soft drinks contain sugars, syrups, colorings, and other additives. Of these ingredients, sugar is the most likely to increase the density of a soft drink. Sugar density can be roughly measured with a simple calibrated hydrometer. The denser the liquid from dissolved sugar, the higher a hydrometer floats. This is because a dense liquid exerts more pressure and pushes up more strongly on the hydrometer.

## Procedure
We fill two glasses with 12 fluid ounces (360 ml) of soft drink and water. A hydrometer reading is made from both glasses. We add sugar, 1 teaspoon (5 ml) at a time, to the water until the water has the same sugar density as the soft drink. Equal densities are shown when the hydrometer floats at the same level in each liquid.

## Hypothesis
About five teaspoons of sugar will be added to a 12-fluid-ounce (360-ml) glass of water to bring it up to the density of the 12-fluid-ounce (360-ml) can of soft drink.

## Experiment to Test Hypothesis
**1.** Open a can of soft drink and pour it into the first glass. Allow the soft drink to sit overnight so that all the carbonation goes out of it. A bubbling soda will give you an inaccurate hydrometer reading.

**2.** Use the measuring cup to pour 12 fluid ounces (360 ml) of water into the second glass.

**3.** Place the hydrometer into the soft drink and note the millimeter level at which it floats.

**4.** Place the hydrometer into the water and compare the level.

**5.** Add 1 teaspoon (5 ml) of sugar to the water, carefully stir, and observe the hydrometer level. Continue adding teaspoons of sugar until the hydrometer floats at the same millimeter level it did in the soft drink.

## Results & Conclusions

Initially, the hydrometer floated a full 5 millimeters higher in the soft drink than it did in the water. Adding 1 teaspoon (5 ml) of sugar had a negligible effect. In fact, only after 10 teaspoons (50 ml) of sugar did the hydrometer gain about 1 millimeter. Twenty more teaspoons (for a total of 30 teaspoons, or 150 ml of sugar) brought the hydrometer to the same level as it was in the soft drink, indicating that the two liquids now had the same densities. The initial hypothesis woefully underestimated the amount of sugar a soft drink contains.

This project demonstrates that a typical 12-fluid-ounce (360-ml) can of soft drink contains as much as 30 teaspoons (150 ml) of sugar!

# Milk Separation

**Adult Help Required**

*How can we separate milk into water and fat components and compare the quantity of each?*

---

## Materials
- 1 cup (240 ml) whole milk
- resealable plastic bag
- superabsorbent polymer crystals (cross-linked polyacrylamide copolymer flakes, available in science supply stores)
- tablespoon
- bowl
- adult helper

**Caution:** *Do not discard polymer crystal material down the sink, garbage disposal, or toilet because the swelling action of the crystals can damage plumbing. Discard in the trash can only.*

## Background
Milk, cream, yogurt, and other dairy products are a homogenized combination of fat and water. Although fat and water will not ordinarily mix, they can be combined or homogenized by adding an emulsifier. An *emulsifier* is a substance that breaks fat into tiny droplets that can mix invisibly with the water. The emulsifier also keeps the fat droplets from sticking together again.

Polymer crystals are useful to scientists because they can absorb up to 300 times their weight in water. In fact, polymer crystals absorb only water,

which makes them useful for this project.

## Procedure
We pour 1 cup (240 ml) of milk in a resealable plastic bag and add 1 tablespoon (15 ml) of polymer crystals. The milk is mixed with the crystals by kneading the bag, and the bag is left overnight.

## Hypothesis
The liquid milk will become a dry powder.

## Experiment to Test Hypothesis
**1.** Pour 1 cup (240 ml) of milk into the resealable bag.

**2.** Add 1 tablespoon (15 ml) of polymer crystals.

**3.** Seal the bag and knead the milk and crystals for about 2 minutes.

**4.** Place the bag where it won't be disturbed and leave overnight.

**5.** Carefully unseal the bag, pour the contents into a bowl, and observe the results.

## Results & Conclusions

The polymer crystals had an interesting and unexpected effect on the milk that was not anticipated in the original hypothesis. Instead of a powder, what remained of the milk was a buttery goo mixed with transparent jellylike chunks. The goo was the butterfat, left behind when the crystals absorbed all the water in the milk. The crystals were clear and jellylike because they had absorbed three times their weight in water. Since there were many more jellylike crystals than butterfat, this project showed that milk is mostly water.

# Swirls in Milk

*How can we determine that milk is a combination of substances that do not ordinarily mix?*

## Materials
- 1 cup (240 ml) whole milk or Half & Half
- red food coloring
- blue food coloring
- shallow bowl or saucer
- vegetable oil
- eyedropper

## Background
Milk, cream, yogurt, and other dairy products are mostly water but also contain a significant amount of fat. Although fat and water are *immiscible* (do not mix), they are blended together by a substance in the milk called an *emulsifier*. This means that you can't really see the fat in milk, although it's certainly there and contributes to the milk's flavor.

## Procedure
We pour milk into a shallow bowl and add drops of red and blue food coloring at the sides of the bowl. A drop of oil is placed in the middle of the bowl and the resulting reaction of milk, color, and oil is observed.

## Hypothesis
The food coloring will move around in the bowl.

## Experiment to Test Hypothesis
1. Pour the cup (240 ml) of milk into the shallow bowl. Make sure the bowl won't be disturbed.

2. With the eyedropper, add a few drops of red food coloring to the sides of the bowl. Repeat with the blue food coloring.

3. Wash out the eyedropper and then carefully add 1 drop of vegetable oil to the center of the bowl.

4. Observe what happens.

## Results & Conclusions
A few seconds after adding the oil, the food coloring began to swirl away from the sides of the bowl in a counterclockwise spiraling pattern. The blue and red mixed in places to create different shades of violet, especially near the center where the drop of oil was added. The motion of the color suggested that the oil, mixing with the fat in the milk, created a current at the milk's surface that was marked by the food coloring.

This current spiraled in a counterclockwise direction due to the *Coriolis effect*, a circular motion that replicates the rotation of Earth in the Northern Hemisphere.

# Woolly Oxygen Indicator

*How can we demonstrate that ordinary air is about 20% oxygen?*

## Materials
- "pinch" of steel wool
- widemouthed jar
- test tube or clear-glass narrow medicine vial
- ruler
- rubber band
- vinegar
- paper cup
- paper towel
- tweezers
- rubber gloves

## Background
Scientists know that ordinary air is composed primarily of three gases—nitrogen, oxygen, and argon. Of the three, nitrogen makes up about 78% of our atmosphere; oxygen about 21%; and argon less than 1%. Other gases—such as carbon dioxide and methane—exist in trace amounts of under one-tenth of 1%, although the amount of carbon dioxide in our atmosphere has been increasing due to industrial pollution. Although it's relatively complicated to measure the amount of nitrogen and argon in our atmosphere, measuring oxygen can be accomplished with a few household materials combined in a simple experiment involving oxidation, or rust.

## Procedure
A small amount of steel wool is pushed into a test tube, which is placed, upside down, in a jar of water.

## Hypothesis
The steel wool will rust, and this reaction requires the presence of oxygen. The volume of oxygen used in this reaction will be measurable and will indicate the overall percentage of oxygen in ordinary air.

## Experiment to Test Hypothesis
1. Use the ruler to measure the length of the test tube and divide that measurement by 5. Take that number (the quotient) and measure it from the bottom of the tube, twisting the rubber band around the tube as a marker. The rubber band marker shows 20% of the tube's volume.

2. Steel wool can cause splinters, so put on the rubber gloves to roll the pinch of wool into a ball the size of a marble.

3. Put the steel wool in the paper cup and pour just enough vinegar into the cup to cover it. Let it soak for about 5 minutes.

**4.** Fill the widemouthed jar with about 1 inch (2.54 cm) of water.

**5.** Remove the steel wool from the vinegar and place it on the paper towel until dry.

**6.** Use the tweezers to push the steel wool into the middle of the test tube so that it's suspended there.

**7.** Put the test tube, opened side down, into the jar with water.

**8.** Leave the jar and test tube undisturbed for a few hours and observe the results.

### Results & Conclusions

It was clear after only an hour that something was happening inside the test tube. The water from the jar was being drawn up inside the tube, and this seemed to be related to the amount of rust appearing on the steel wool. Placing the tube inside the jar trapped the air in the tube so that the mysterious reaction could be clearly observed. The steel wool was oxidizing (rusting) because some of its iron atoms combined with oxygen atoms.

Rust forms only when oxygen is present. When oxygen atoms are in a gaseous state, they take up much more space than when the same atoms combine to form solid rust. As a result of oxygen's change from gas to solid (helped by first soaking the wool in vinegar), a vacuum was formed in the tube that reduced the tube's air pressure. Like the workings of a barometer, the higher atmospheric pressure outside pushed water into the tube.

But the best part of this project was watching how the water was drawn up no farther than the rubber-band marker on the test tube—the 20% line! The hypothesis was correct: No matter how long the wool was left to rust, no more than 20% oxygen was available in ordinary air to facilitate the process.

Interestingly, the amount of oxygen in our atmosphere varies from place to place on the surface of Earth. This is due mainly to the presence of aerosols—tiny particles in the form of droplets, dust, ice crystals, smoke, or volcanic emissions—suspended in the air—all of which reduce the level of oxygen. Humidity also affects the amount of oxygen present.

# Seven

# SKY *Watch*

# Balloon Model Universe

*Can the interval or distance ratio of an expanding universe be simulated by inflating a dotted balloon?*

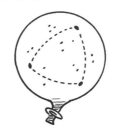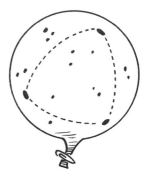

## Materials
- large balloon (dark blue or black, if possible)
- white correction fluid
- paper clip
- red, yellow, and green permanent markers
- tape measure
- pen
- paper (to record measurements)
- strong lungs

## Background
The idea that we live in an expanding universe is one of the strangest and most important discoveries of 20th century science. For thousands of years, everyone, including astronomers, had assumed that the universe was a stable, unchanging place where astronomical events played themselves out. But in the 1910s and 1920s, several physicists and astronomers made discoveries that defied easy explanation. These discoveries came together in the mind of an astronomer named Edwin Hubble, who explained it all in 1929 with his *expanding-universe* theory.

Hubble's theory suggested that the entire universe started from a single explosion called the Big Bang. Hubble created a diagram to help explain his theory. It showed that, since the Big Bang, the universe is expanding uniformly so that the distance between every two galaxies grows by the same fraction for every time interval. This will be demonstrated with our balloon model universe.

## Procedure
A balloon is inflated halfway and then painted with correcting-fluid dots representing galaxies. The distances between three galaxies in a triangular configuration are measured, the balloon inflated further, and the distances measured again.

## Hypothesis
The distances measured between galaxies will grow by the same fraction in every time interval, according to Hubble's expanding-universe theory.

## Experiment to Test Hypothesis
**1.** Blow up the balloon until it's firm but small. Pinch the bottom shut with the paper clip.

**2.** Use the correcting fluid to dot the surface of the balloon, making some dots a little larger than the others. The dots can be random, but their arrangement should look somewhat galaxylike.

**3.** After the correcting fluid dries, choose three large galaxies on one side of your balloon and color them red, yellow, and green.

**4.** Measure the distance between the red and yellow galaxies, yellow and green galaxies, and green and red galaxies. Your measurements should trace out a triangle.

**5.** Measure the distance between your green galaxy and a distant white galaxy on the other side of your balloon. Color the white galaxy green, also.

**6.** Remove the paper clip and blow five times into the balloon. Pinch the balloon shut and measure the distance between the red and yellow galaxies again. Stop blowing and tie the balloon closed when the distance is double what it was for your first measurement.

**7.** Measure the distances between the galaxies that make up your triangle again. Then measure the distance between the large green galaxy and the smaller one on the other side of the balloon. Record all measurements and compare them.

### Results & Conclusions

When our balloon was only half-inflated, the distance between the red galaxy and yellow galaxy was 3⅝ inches (9.2 cm); between yellow and green 2 inches (5 cm), and between green and red 2¼ inches (5.7 cm). The distance between the green galaxy and its distant green cousin was 5 inches (12.7 cm). The large galaxies traced out an obtuse triangle, with one angle of the triangle noticeably

larger than 90°. This was the angle made by the green galaxy with its neighboring red and yellow galaxies.

The balloon was inflated and measurements taken again until the original distance between the red and yellow galaxies had doubled. At this point, distances between all other colored galaxies were remeasured. True to our predictions, the doubling of distance between the red and yellow galaxies was true for all the other galaxies as well. This meant that the distances had doubled between all galaxies on the surface of the balloon and that our balloon universe had expanded uniformly in the "time interval" of inflation. We tested this by measuring the distance between the green galaxy and its distant cousin. Here the distance was not quite doubled, which may have reflected the fact that the skin closer to the mouth of the balloon (where the small green galaxy was) didn't expand as much as the rest of the balloon.

Our balloon represents a two-dimensional universe instead of a three-dimensional one. Beings living in our balloon universe would only travel across the surface of the balloon. This means that the inside and outside of the balloon represent a dimension inaccessible to them—time. The air inside the balloon represents the past for this universe; the air surrounding it represents the future. In a similar way, the expansion of our universe in three dimensions is only part of the story because we cannot directly experience the fourth dimension of time.

# Comets in a Pan

*Is it possible to simulate the movement
and gassy streams of comets by floating pieces
of dry ice in warm water?*

## Materials
- large, black-coated (Teflon or T-Fal) frying pan
- dry ice
- thick towel
- hammer
- tweezers
- warm water
- adult helper

**Caution:** *Dry ice is the frozen form of carbon dioxide. The ice has an extremely low temperature and should never come in contact with bare skin.*

## Background

Comets—among the most spectacular sights of the heavens—are irregularly shaped bodies composed of dust and frozen gases. They have highly elliptical orbits that bring them very close to the sun and swing them deeply into space, often beyond the orbit of Pluto, where they leave our solar system and usually never return. The structures of comets vary, but all comets have a cloud of material called a *coma* that surrounds an icy *nucleus*.

The nucleus is usually very small, less than 10 kilometers (about 6.2 miles), but the coma can elongate millions of miles as the comet approaches the sun.

When far from the sun, a comet's nucleus is very cold and the material inside is frozen solid. This is what astronomers call the dirty-snowball stage of the comet, since, at this time, the comet is composed mostly of ice. But when a comet comes within several Astronomical Units of the sun, the surface of the nucleus begins to warm, and the frozen material sublimes, which means that it goes directly from a solid to a gaseous state. The streaming away of sublimed material in a luminous plume is what gives a comet its spectacular tail. But in reality, most comets have two tails—one made of gassy plasma and the other composed of microscopic dust particles. The tails of the comet are pushed by the solar wind, which means that they always point away from the sun, even if the comet itself is moving away from the sun.

This project simulates only basic comet principles—mainly, the sublimation of solid ice into a gassy plume.

*A single Astronomical Unit (AU) is measured as the mean distance from Earth to the sun: 149,597,870 km or 92,960,116 miles, or roughly 93,000,000 miles.*

*1 mile = 1.6093 kilometers*
*1 kilometer = 0.6214 mile*

## Procedure

Small pieces of dry ice are placed in a pan of warm water and the sublimation of ice into gas is observed, noting the parallel to basic comet chemistry.

## Hypothesis

The pieces of dry ice will sublime into streams, plumes, and eddies that will simulate the coma of a comet.

## Experiment to Test Hypothesis

**1.** Fill the pan to about 1 inch (2.54 cm) deep with warm tap water.

**2.** With an adult's help, wrap the piece of dry ice in a thick towel and use the hammer to break the ice through the towel. Smash the ice until it feels almost flat.

**3.** Open the towel and use the tweezers to select a few small pieces of dry ice, none larger than ¼ inch (0.635 cm) in diameter. If your piece floats when you drop it in the water, it's too big.

**4.** Observe what happens shortly after you drop the pieces of dry ice in the pan of water. Gently blow across the water and watch what happens.

## Results & Conclusions

Only seconds after dropping the pieces of ice, they darted around the surface of the water trailing a plume of carbon-dioxide gas. An irregularly shaped piece would sometimes spin, the gas assuming a whirlpool shape. Two pieces of dry ice that approached each other would stick together, unless the plume of one pushed the other away.

But the most dramatic effect came when blowing across the surface of the water. The plumes from all pieces of ice turned, like compass needles, in the direction of the wind. This clearly demonstrated the effect of solar wind on the coma of a comet.

As in a comet, the solid ice sublimed, meaning that it turned directly into a gas. But unlike a true comet, the pieces of dry ice were propelled directionally by the gas streaming behind them.

# A DVD Spectroscope

**Adult Help Required**

*Is a possible to construct a spectroscope out of everyday materials that will successfully demonstrate the process of stellar spectral analysis?*

## Materials

- DVD or compact disk (disposable)
- shoe box (or similar box)
- 2 single-edge razor blades (scraper style, found in hardware stores)
- cardboard tube (from a toilet-paper roll)
- cellophane tape
- masking tape
- marker
- craft knife
- ruler
- adult helper

**Caution:** *This project requires using a craft knife to cut cardboard and 2 scraper-style razor blades to make a slit. These tools should be handled by an adult.*

## Background

A spectroscope is an optical instrument that helps astronomers see what something is made of. When a material is heated to incandescence, it emits light that is characteristic of the atomic makeup of the material. The resulting spectrum can consist of either bright emission bands or dark absorption *Fraunhofer lines*. This configuration of bands and lines is unique to the atoms, molecules, or ions that comprise the substance. By using a spectroscope, astronomers can determine the chemical composition of a distant star simply by examining its spectrum and measuring the various wavelengths.

The basic parts of a spectroscope are a slit and collimator (lens) for producing a parallel beam, a prism or diffraction grating for fanning out a viewable spectrum, and a telescope, camera, or viewing tube. The tube is sometimes placed at an angle to make the spectrum easier to see. If a camera is used to record the spectrum, the device is known as a spectro*graph*. (Today all spectroscopes are actually spectrographs since observations are no longer made visually.) When the science of making diffraction gratings was perfected, the gratings quickly replaced the heavy and expensive prisms that were used in earlier spectroscopes. The gratings, made up of thousands of prismatic ledges edged onto a flat sheet, allowed for smaller and lighter spectroscopes.

Through spectroscopy we know the stuff of stars. The spectroscope shows us that the universe is expanding and the galaxies are receding. It also shows us that there are other stars in the universe very much like our sun—stars that might support solar systems similar to our own.

## Procedure

We construct a simple spectroscope consisting of three main parts: a slit made from razor blades (collimator), a diffraction grating made from the DVD, and a viewing tube of cardboard. The materials are assembled into a usable instrument that should produce clear spectrums for the substances tungsten, mercury, and sodium-neon.

## Hypothesis

Three distinctly different spectrums will be viewed through the spectroscope, each unique to the incandescent substances that created it.

## Experiment to Test Hypothesis

**1.** For your spectroscope to operate properly, all three parts must be carefully aligned. Remove the cover of the shoe box and turn the box on its narrow side with the top of the box facing away from you. Place the DVD in the bottom left corner of the side facing you, then move the DVD ½ inch (1.25 cm) from the left edge of the box. Trace the inside circle of the DVD on the box.

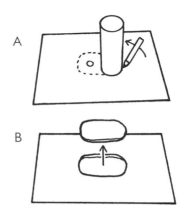

A

B

**2.** Center the cardboard tube over the circle you just traced. Now trace around the tube so that you have two circles, one inside the other. Move the tube ½ inch (1.25 cm) to the right and trace around it again. An oval shape results from the combined tracing. Cut out this shape with the craft knife.

**3.** Turn the box on its right side so that the cut out part is to your right. Place the DVD against the left edge of this side and trace another small circle. This circle will be used as a guide only.

**4.** At the far left edge, cut a rectangle. The rectangle should begin as a small square at the same height as the circle you traced from the DVD. Turn the square into a rectangle by elongating the top and bottom so that you wind up with a cutout area ½ inch (1.25 cm) wide by 2 inches (5 cm) wide.

**5.** Place the two scraper razor blades over the rectangular area so that their sharp edges almost touch. Use cellophane tape to attach the blades to the box, being careful to leave an even gap between the sharp edges, not one that's wider at the top or bottom.

**6.** Turn the box right side up with the slit facing you. Tape the CD disk onto the back wall of the box. The rainbow side should face you. (You can keep the DVD surface unspoiled by making tape loops and pressing them against the back of the disk). Check your alignment by making sure that the left edge of the disk and the slit are the same distance from the edge of the box.

**7.** Put the cover on the box and use the masking tape to seal up any places where light might leak into the box and spoil the spectrum.

**8.** Place the cardboard tube in the cutout hole at an angle facing away from the slit. Pick up the box and take it outdoors so that light comes through the slit. Move the tube slightly until you see a clear spectrum ranging from red to violet. Tape the tube at whatever angle produces the best spectrum. Seal all spaces around the tube with masking tape to keep light from leaking in.

**9.** Bring the finished spectroscope indoors and place an ordinary incandescent lightbulb near the slit. Observe the spectrum through the tube. Place the slit near a fluorescent light and compare results. Try out the spectroscope on neon and argon (low-light streetlamps).

## Results & Conclusions

The fine laser-etched surface of the DVD worked as an excellent diffraction grating and produced a wide, fan-shaped spectrum for each test. The incandescent bulb showed a basic color spectrum with no bright lines. This is because the light was radiating from a hot solid—the glowing tungsten filament inside the bulb—rather than from a glowing gas.

The fluorescent light produced something entirely different. Here, the heated mercury vapor produced a spectrum with bright Fraunhofer lines in green, orange, and violet—a spectral pattern typical of glowing mercury.

After dark we approached the nearest streetlight and observed the fuzzy reddish-orange spectrum of sodium and neon—two elements that combine and vaporize to create the pinkish color of the streetlight.

With a little practice, it would be entirely possible to recognize the signature spectrum for various elements and so recognize the chemical composition of an apparently unknown incandescent gas. In this way, astronomers can reach across the heavens and unravel some of the mysteries of distant stars and galaxies.

# Ejecta Patterns of Craters

*Can some typical ejecta (i.e., material thrown out, as in a volcanic eruption) patterns of craters, such as those observed on the moon, be reproduced by dropping objects of various sizes and weights into salt?*

## Materials

- 10 cups (2.4 L) salt
- fine-ground pepper or powdered cocoa
- large shallow plastic dish (used under potted plants)
- black posterboard
- cardboard tube (from paper towel roll)
- glass marble or ball bearing
- small fishing weight
- pebbles in assorted sizes
- teaspoon
- scissors
- ruler
- camera
- spray varnish (optional)

**Note:** *If you choose to follow optional Step 11, use pepper rather than cocoa.*

## Background

Craters are the most common feature on the surfaces of most planets. The moon's prominent crater Copernicus is not only beautiful, but it clearly displays the shape, shadings, and distinct patterns of impact ejecta that characterize all craters to one degree or another. When an object hits the surface of a planet, the object completely vaporizes, releasing energy in an explosion that sprays debris in a circular pattern and leaves behind the typical bowl shape of the crater. This explosion is millions of times greater than that of the most powerful land mine.

Earth, too, has its craters, but because our planet is so meteorologically and geologically active, most of Earth's craters have been removed by forces of weather and erosion. Still, new surprises about Earth craters turn up periodically. Near Sudbury, Ontario, Canada, scientists discovered a crater that was formed when a mountain-size meteor hit Earth about 1.8 billion years ago. This space rock, colliding with Earth at a speed of 89,000 mph (40 kps), was so huge that it essentially turned part of Earth's mantle inside out, leaving a crater that measures roughly 37 miles (60 km) long, 19 miles (30 km) wide, and 9 miles (15 km) deep.

The following project seeks to create slightly more modest craters using various projectiles in salt.

## Procedure

A marble, fishing weight, and pebbles of various sizes are dropped into salt to observe the patterns and distances of impact ejecta. Objects are dropped at various angles to see if different ejecta patterns result.

## Hypothesis

Each object will create a crater of a slightly different shape. The angle at which objects are dropped will affect the size and shape of the craters. In all cases, craters will be much larger than the objects that create them.

## Experiment to Test Hypothesis

**1.** Place the shallow plastic planting dish on a level surface and add 10 cups (2.4 L) of salt (more or less), making sure that the salt is about 2 inches (5 cm) deep.

**2.** Using the teaspoon as a shovel, build up the salt at the center to make a small mound that's roughly even with the sides of the dish. Flatten the top of this mound with the edge of the ruler.

**3.** Cut a hole about 4 inches (10 cm) in diameter at the center of the posterboard. (You can find the center by connecting opposite corners in diagonal lines—where they cross indicates the center.) Place the posterboard over the planting dish so that the level mound shows through the hole.

**4.** Hold the paper-towel cardboard tube over the salt to center your ball bearing, which should be dropped from a height of about 10 inches (25 cm). Drop the ball bearing through the tube and observe it hitting the exposed salt. Photograph the pattern of ejecta formed on the surrounding black posterboard.

**5.** Remove the posterboard, smooth the mound of salt, and repeat Step 4, this time using the fishing weight and pebbles. Photograph and compare ejecta patterns of each drop.

**6.** Remove the posterboard, and use the ruler to level the sand around the dish. After you make the surface as smooth as possible, sprinkle a thin layer of pepper on the salt. The layer should completely cover the salt, but not too thickly.

**7.** With the tube guiding you, drop the ball bearing into the salt. Observe the resulting crater and photograph it. Drop the ball bearing again, but this time from a height of 1 yard (about 1 meter). Observe this crater and how it impacts the first crater.

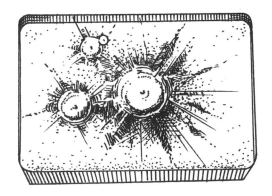

*1 yard = 36 inches*
*1 meter = 39.37 inches*
*1 yard = 0.9144 meter*

**8.** If your salt can be cleaned by raking it free of the scattered pepper, proceed to the next step. If the salt is permanently discolored, use the teaspoon to shovel away the top layer and add fresh salt, covering it with a layer of pepper as before.

**9.** Drop the fishing weight and pebbles into the salt, at various heights, each time noting the results. Photograph the more interesting crater formations you create.

**10.** Rake the salt clean, and finish off by dropping all objects at various angles into the salt. The more extreme the angle, the better. See if this variation of dropping technique changes the shape and quality of your craters.

**11.** *Optional:* If you want to preserve your craters and ejecta patterns, coat them with several layers of spray varnish. Three or four coats of varnish—with a couple of hours drying between each coat—will create a rigid (though delicate) crust that can be removed for display. (Don't try this if you've used powdered cocoa, however. The cocoa melts into a sticky goo that blurs your patterns.)

## Results & Conclusions

The surprising result of this project was that most of the craters—regardless of what object was dropped and from what height—looked pretty much the same (perfect circles), although they varied in size. This contradicted the part of the hypothesis stating that each object would create a differently shaped crater. In fact, the only differences between craters were the larger sprays of ejecta when objects were dropped from greater heights. The first posterboard drop resulted in a ring of ejecta with a radius of about four inches. The higher drop threw ejecta out a full foot from impact, with some of it even going beyond the posterboard. But in both cases, the rings of ejecta were almost perfect circles.

This was not the case when objects were dropped at different angles. Dropped at an angle low to the surface, the object's ejecta didn't spread out in a symmetrical pattern but continued on in the direction of impact. This created a "fan" of ejecta on one side of the crater, which had a slightly oblong shape. Examining the bowl of each crater revealed powder lines on the crater walls. These were formed shortly after impact when debris slid back down into the crater.

One part of our hypothesis was entirely supported, however. In all cases, the craters were much larger than the objects that created them. Each crater had a diameter about 10 times that of the ball bearing, weight, or pebble that created it.

# Gravity Well Game

*Is it possible to simulate the attraction of mass in a gravity well with the aid of a trampoline and a cooperative friend?*

## Materials
- backyard trampoline
- 10 croquet balls
- chalk
- a rather large friend

## Background
Besides keeping us from flying off the face of the Earth, gravity also pulls things up and sideways. For example, the moon's gravity causes the ocean tides to rise, and the sun pulls the orbiting Earth toward it.

According to Einstein's general theory of relativity, gravity isn't like some giant magnet, but something much more interesting. Einstein thought that gravity was actually a distortion of space due to a concentration of matter. The greater the concentration of matter, the more distorted the space around it and the stronger the gravitational attraction. This is why the Earth tugs at you more than you tug at the Earth. And this is also why planets pull things toward themselves, like meteors.

This project—actually a kind of game—demonstrates how the space around something massive can be distorted.

## Procedure
The heavier of two players sits in the center of a trampoline that has been marked with concentric circles, each with a point value. Croquet balls are rolled across the trampoline to see which player can accumulate more points.

## Hypothesis
The trampoline, distorted in the center from the weight of the sitting friend, will effectively mimic the behavior of matter in a gravity well.

## Experiment to Test Hypothesis
**1.** Use a medium-size backyard trampoline if you have access to one; otherwise the trampoline at your school might be available after the last gym period.

**2.** Starting at the center of the trampoline and using chalk, draw a circle just a little wider than your friend's backside (you may need a tape measure for this).

**3.** Draw a second circle around the first circle, leaving about 8 inches (20 cm) between the circles.

**4.** Draw two more circles, each one about 8 inches (20 cm) more in diameter than the previous one, until you reach the edge of the trampoline. You should have a total of five circles.

**5.** Leave the center circle blank. In a row starting from the left edge of the trampoline, write the point numbers 2, 4, 6, and 8.

**6.** Walk to the opposite side of the trampoline and write the numbers again, starting from the left edge. You should have a long row of numbers across the trampoline, half of them upside down.

**7.** Have your large friend carefully (to avoid smearing the chalk) climb into the first unnumbered circle and sit there, cross-legged.

**8.** With your croquet balls near you, stand at the left edge of the trampoline. Your competitor should stand on the other side of the trampoline so that each of you sees the numbers correctly.

**9.** Begin the game by rolling a croquet ball across the trampoline. Since you collect points for each circle your ball passes through, aim your ball as close to the center circle as you can. But be careful! If your ball rolls too close to the center, it'll get sucked into your sitting friend's "gravitation" and bump him. When this happens, you lose all points for that turn.

**10.** Total up each player's score after five rolls. The player with the higher score wins.

## Results & Conclusions

Our sitting friend was an effective massive object whose gravity well predictably sucked most of our rolling balls into his lap. Even balls rolled forcefully toward the outer circles (with the strategy that the higher of two low scores would still be a winning score) were quickly accelerated toward the inside where they bumped our friend.

In reality, a gravity well exists in three-dimensional space. Even though our game occurs on the two-dimensional surface of the trampoline, it still successfully demonstrated the gravitational pull of massive objects.

# The Green Flash—Truth or Fiction?

*Does the so-called green flash seen immediately after a bright red sunset actually exist?*

## Materials
- 8½x11 inch (21x27.5 cm) thick white paper
- markers or crayons in red, yellow, blue, and black
- ruler
- pencil compass

## Background
At the end of a long summer day, particularly when the air is clear and a spectacular sunset is promised, people along coastal areas wait to see something called the green flash. The flash is a moment of bright green that supposedly lights up a bell-shaped patch of sky over the horizon right after the sun disappears. Although fairly well known, no one has come up with a plausible explanation for the flash. Some believe it's a form of light refraction that occurs only under certain atmospheric conditions. Others claim that the flash is more of an illusion created by the retinal afterimage of our own eyes. This project seeks to explore the second theory.

## Procedure
A subject stares at a paper with two brightly colored representations of a sky—one of sunset and the other directly after sunset. Afterimages of the representations are described.

## Hypothesis
The subject will see a green flash in the after-sunset sky.

## Experiment to Test Hypothesis
**1.** Fold the paper in half, top edge to bottom edge.

**2.** On the half facing you, measure 2 inches (5 cm) from the bottom edge and draw a horizontal line in black across the page. Make an X at the middle of the line.

**3.** Open the compass to 2 inches (5 cm) and place the needle on the X.

**4.** Sweep the compass over the line so that you have a half-circle.

**5.** Color the inside of the half-circle red and the outside yellow.

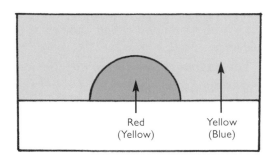

Red (Yellow)     Yellow (Blue)

**6.** Open the paper and repeat Steps 2 through 4. Color the inside of this half-circle yellow and the outside blue.

**7.** Fold the paper so that the red half-circle faces you. Stare at the X for one full minute, allowing the rest of the half-circle to enter your peripheral vision only. (Ask a friend to keep time for you.)

**8.** After a minute, open the paper *without moving your eyes*, so that you are now staring at the yellow half-circle.

### Results & Conclusions

When we switched our stare from the red half-circle to the yellow half-circle, the yellow turned a bright green, which tapered off into the blue surrounding area—a green flash! The flash persisted for a few seconds but then dissipated when we moved our eyes. However, wherever we looked for the next 3 minutes seemed to take on a greenish hue.

The explanation can be found in something called the retinal afterimage. Light is perceived in the part of the eye called the retina. The retina is covered with light-sensitive cells called rods and cones, each set of which has a specific function. The rods are useful for night vision because they are sensitive to shades of gray. The cones, on the other hand, are useful for day vision because they sense color.

Staring at a particular color, say red, for too long fatigues the red-sensitive cones in the retina because they are forced to continually send the electrochemical signal "red" to the brain. When the red disappears, the cones "relax" by producing a signal for green, the complementary color of red. If the color yellow exhausts the cones, they relax by producing blue. The phenomenon of color afterimage means that whichever color fatigues the cones of the eye will cause them to produce the complementary color.

When the sky is lit brilliant red by the setting sun—particularly if the red is reflected in the ocean—the cones of the eye are literally blasted with red. This is compounded if the viewer is looking directly at the setting sun. *Never* a good idea! Cones, stunned by red, are eager to relax at the first opportunity. That opportunity occurs when the sun drops below the horizon and the intensity of the sky's color diminishes.

A sun gone below the horizon doesn't produce a white sky, but it does produce one with considerably less reds or oranges and deeper blues. Combine this background of blue with the sudden retinal afterimage of green and you have perfect conditions for the green flash.

## An Alternate View

Since no one has definitively proved or disproved the existence of the flash, an alternate explanation is worth looking at. This theory (and others like it) interprets the flash as an actual optical event caused by the refraction of light over the horizon.

After leaving the vacuum of space and entering our atmosphere, light from the sun slows down a little and bends downward. (This is the same effect as when the lower half of a spoon bends down in a glass of water.) At sunrise or sunset, the bending down of sunlight causes an image of the sun to appear above its actual position on the horizon. This image, as it slips behind a thicker slice of atmosphere, is separated into the various colors that make up white light—a phenomenon called *chromatic aberration*.

The degree of aberration depends on the wavelength of the light. Blue light bends more than red light. Other colors will bend more or less depending on their wavelengths. But the chromatic aberration of a setting sun will always take the form of a red fringe around the sun's bottom and a greenish-blue one at the top. As the sun sinks below the horizon, the reds at the bottom are blocked by Earth, leaving only the blues and greens at the top. For an instant, these colors seem to fill a low area on the horizon, just before the sun drops out of sight. This is the green flash.

# How Big Is Mars?

*Starting with two clay balls with equal diameters, how can the volume of the balls be combined so that one ball winds up with half the diameter of the other ball—the comparative sizes of Earth and Mars?*

## Materials
- modeling clay
- plastic knife
- ruler
- waxed paper

## Background
Our solar system has nine planets that orbit the sun. The closest planet to the sun is Mercury, followed by Venus, Earth, Mars, Jupiter, Saturn, Uranus, Neptune, and far off Pluto. The sizes of the planets vary widely, with the largest—Jupiter— nearly 63 times wider than the smallest—Pluto. Some planets, like Venus and Earth, are nearly the same size. Others, like Mars, are only about half the size of Earth. But size, as this project demonstrates, is not a very accurate way to compare planets.

## Procedure
A chunk of modeling clay is divided into two balls the same size. Clay is removed from one of the balls until the ball accurately reflects the size of Mars as compared to Earth.

## Hypothesis
Since Mars has a diameter half that of Earth's, the Mars ball will have to be divided in half again.

## Experiment to Test Hypothesis
**1.** Put a piece of waxed paper on a tabletop and place the ruler on the paper. Take a chunk of clay and put it next to the ruler. Use the ruler to help you build up your chunk until you have a ball about 2 inches (5 cm) in diameter. Move that ball and make another. One ball will be Earth and the other Mars.

**2.** Roll the Mars ball into a cylinder. Cut that cylinder in half and roll one half into a smaller Mars ball. Place this smaller Mars ball next to the Earth ball and compare diameters, using the ruler. Mars is still too big.

**3.** Cut the cylinder in half again so that you have a quarter of the original cylinder. Roll this into an even smaller Mars ball and compare its diameter to the Earth ball. Even though you're getting closer, Mars is still just a little too big around the waist.

**4.** Finally, cut the quarter cylinder in half so that you have one-eighth of the original cylinder. Roll this into a Mars ball and compare it with the Earth ball. Finally, you have two balls that seem to accurately compare the sizes of Earth and Mars. To prove this, slice the Earth and Mars balls in half and place the two halves of the Mars ball against the half of the Earth ball.

## Results & Conclusions

By Step 2 it was clear that our hypothesis was incorrect and some boning up on geometry was in order. As the project demonstrated, it took eight divisions of the cylinder before we had a Mars ball with one half the diameter of the Earth ball. This reflects the relationship of two properties, volume (V) and radius (R), and is represented by the equation $V = \frac{4}{3} \times R^3$, meaning that the volume of a sphere is proportional to the cube of its radius.

For example, if the Earth ball has a volume of 1, then the Mars ball (with half the diameter and half the radius of the Earth ball) would have a volume of $\frac{4}{3} \times (\frac{1}{2})^3$ which equals one-eighth the volume of the Earth ball. Since we started out with two balls the same size, it was interesting to note that we had to divide one of them into eight parts before creating a ball that accurately represented the size of Mars.

# Meteoritic Sand

*Is it possible to find micrometeorites in ordinary beach sand?*

## Materials
- neodymium magnet (available at science supply stores)
- zip-tight plastic bag
- pail
- water
- cone-shaped coffee filter
- large jar
- masking tape
- scissors
- magnifying glass

## Background
Meteorites, or the pieces of space rock that fall to Earth, tell astronomers much about the birth of the universe. But finding good specimens, especially in populated areas, can be a challenge. For this reason, serious meteorite hunters regularly travel to places like the South Pole, where winds of up to 200 miles (322 km) per hour blow meteorites across sheets of ice. The meteorites collect at the base of mountains where they're easily recognized.

But meteorites, at least very small ones, are all around—even in the most ordinary places, like the beach. Called *micrometeors*, they are too small and too light to burn up as they enter Earth's atmosphere so they remain floating in the air. Some fall to the ground only when attached to tiny water droplets or dust particles.

Micrometeor particles have a unique rounded shape that distinguishes them from Earth-originated particles, such as magnetic magnetite. Like larger meteors, however, micrometeors can be either metallic or rocky and are mostly made up of debris left by comets and stellar explosions. That's why the best time to go micrometeor hunting is shortly after a meteor shower. The chart below lists the major showers and when they occur each year. The hourly rates are those for a single observer.

## Major Meteor Showers Chart

| Shower | Date Observed | Hourly Rate |
| --- | --- | --- |
| Quadrantids | January 3 | 40 |
| Lyrids | April 21 | 15 |
| Aquarids | May 4 | 20 |
| Perseids | August 11 | 50 |
| Orionids | October 21 | 25 |
| Taurids | November 4 | 15 |
| Leonids | November 16 | 15 |
| Geminids | December 13 | 50 |
| Ursids | December 22 | 15 |

This project will use simple tools—a magnet placed in a zip-tight bag—to hunt for metallic micrometeors at the beach. Our findings will be observed under a magnifying glass.

## Procedure
We place a strong neodymium magnet in a zip-tight bag that's sealed and dragged through beach sand. The bag is removed from the sand, dipped into water, and the magnet taken out so that the particles can fall to the bottom. The water is decanted from the pail with the aid of a coffee filter, and the particles, once dry, are examined with a magnifying glass.

## Hypothesis
Although many magnetic particles will be extracted from the sand, only some will show the unique shape of micrometeorites.

## Experiment to Test Hypothesis
**1.** Go to the beach, or collect sand from a beach, shortly after a major meteor shower.

**2.** Put the neodymium magnet inside a zip-tight bag and seal the bag tightly so that nothing can get inside. Drag the bag through the sand, making sure that sand covers all sides of the bag.

**3.** Remove the bag from the sand, fill a pail one-third full of water, and carefully push the bag under the water. Open the bag and slowly remove the magnet so that whatever is stuck to the outside falls away.

**4.** Tape a coffee filter to the mouth of the large jar, and slowly pour the water through the coffee filter. If the filter becomes clogged with debris, replace it with a fresh filter, but save the old one.

**5.** After you've completely decanted the pail, place the debris-coated coffee filters where they can dry out. Use the scissors to carefully cut open the filters so that you can spread them flat.

**6.** When the filters are completely dry, examine the debris with the magnifying glass, looking for unusual shapes and sizes.

## Results & Conclusions
Most of the gathered particles looked rocky and crystalline—almost like black salt. Some were reddish or deep brown. These were probably magnetite and magnetic garnet—both substances of Earthly origins. However, a few particles were distinctly different—blob-shaped and shiny. Some even had a silvery tinge. About two in every ten particles looked like this. Since scientists estimate that about 20% of the magnetic material on Earth's surface is from outer space, it seemed reasonable to conclude that the blob-shaped particles were indeed metallic micrometeors.

# Refraction Patterns of Starlight

*Can the radio-symmetrical patterns of distant starlight be simulated by viewing pinpoints of light through a polyester gradient?*

## Materials
- 1 square yard (0.84 square meter) black or dark blue polyester or nylon organza
- two 14-inch (35-cm) embroidery hoops (smaller is okay)
- 28x22½-inch (70x56-cm) white posterboard
- aluminum foil
- masking tape
- black spray paint
- spray adhesive
- bare lightbulb
- string
- pencil
- pushpin
- newspapers
- scissors
- stapler

## Background
Even through the most powerful telescope, the human eye can't focus on something as far away as a star. Even the closest star to Earth—Proxima Centauri—is a distant 4 light-years from us. To get an idea of just how far away that is, consider that light travels 186,000 miles (300,000 km) per second. Since there are 31,449,600 seconds in a year, and each second represents 186,000 miles, 4 light years translate into a little over 23 trillion miles! This means that even our closest star neighbor is hardly close.

Since stars are so distant, no one can actually see them. Only the radio-symmetrical patterning of starlight is visible to the human eye. This patterning is caused by refraction (the bending of light), and is affected by all manner of things—dust, ice, gases—between you and the star. Distant starlight is also distorted by Earth's many-layered atmosphere. These layers have different thicknesses and are sometimes turbulent, so starlight doesn't travel in a straight line, but rather bends thousands of times per second (we say it twinkles) before it reaches Earth.

This project attempts to simulate the *simple refractive cross pattern* of starlight as seen on a clear winter night.

## Procedure
The cone is made from posterboard, and its narrow end is wrapped around a bare lightbulb. A sheet of aluminum foil is stretched over the wide end of the cone and pinholes are made in the foil. The "stars" are viewed through stretched polyester.

**Hypothesis**

Viewed with the naked eye, the pinpoints of light will appear as luminous dots. Viewed through the gradient, the pinpoints will take on distinct starlike patterns.

**Experiment to Test Hypothesis**

1. Cut a piece of string a little longer than half the length of the posterboard. Tie the pencil to one end of the string.

2. Turn the posterboard horizontally and mark the middle of the bottom edge. Hold the free end of the string over this mark with your index finger, and guided by the taut string, use your other hand to sweep the pencil around in an arc connecting the two bottom corners of the posterboard.

3. Draw another, much smaller arc by shortening the length of the string to 2½ inches (6.35 cm). Cut along the lines you drew so that you wind up with the shape illustrated.

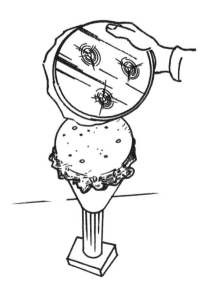

4. Protect your work surface with newspapers. Spray adhesive on one side of the posterboard and cover it with aluminum foil, shiny side up. (The foil doesn't have to be very flat or neat, since this reflective surface will be hidden when you make the cone.) Use the scissors to trim any foil that sticks over the edges of the posterboard.

5. Bend the posterboard into a cone with the foil inside. Keep the cone together by first stapling the corners near the small hole and large opening, then tape the seam of the cone on both sides.

6. Place the wide end of the cone on a sheet of aluminum foil (shiny side up) and tape the edges of the foil to the sides of the cone. You should wind up with a cone having a drumlike covering of dull aluminum foil. Coat the foil with a layer of black spray paint.

7. When the paint dries, use the pushpin to make several holes in the foil. Some holes can be a little larger than others, but avoid making too many holes close together. The pattern of holes should look like a typical starry sky.

8. Cut the nylon organza into two pieces, each slightly larger than its embroidery hoop. Stretch the pieces into their loops, pulling the cloth around the edges to make it as tight and wrinkle-free as possible.

**9.** Remove the shade from a small desk lamp and make sure the bulb is no more than 100 watts. Anything higher will produce too much heat against the posterboard.

**10.** Turn on the lamp and unplug it. Place the opening of the cone over the bare lightbulb, pressing it down until the cone sits securely on the lamp base. You should wind up with a lamp having an upside down "lampshade."

**11.** Find a dark place to test the project. Place the cone on the floor and plug in the lamp. Stand over the foil and look at the pinpoints of light.

**12.** Now look at the lights through one of the embroidery hoops, keeping the hoop about 1 foot (30 cm) from your face. Turn the hoop slowly. Then place the second embroidery hoop over the first and turn them in opposite directions, still watching the stars.

**Results & Conclusions**

With the naked eye, the pinpoint stars appeared as distinct points of light. Some had slight halos around them. These pinpoints might represent actual astronomical objects—such as the closer planets—that can be seen with the naked eye and show only faint radio-symmetrical refraction patterns.

Viewing the pinpoints through the one hoop was an entirely different experience. This time, distinct crosses of light appeared, each one white in the center with rays of orange and blue. The size of the crosses appeared related to the sizes of the holes. Turning the hoop made the crosses all turn together, sometimes resulting in longer vertical rays than horizontal ones, and in different colors appearing.

To simulate the many layers of shifting dust and turbulent atmosphere starlight passes through, we added a second hoop to the first. The two hoops made the refraction patterns much more complicated. Instead of a simple cross, the patterns now had eight shorter rays. When we turned the hoops in opposite directions, one set of four rays seemed to dance around the other set—a truly starlike experience!

# Tiny Earth Light

*If a model globe is oriented properly, will the globe's light and dark sides mimic real-time day and night zones of Earth?*

## Materials

- a model globe of Earth (removed from the stand)
- widemouthed glass jar
- compass
- toothpick
- modeling clay

## Background

Earth rotates around an imaginary line that passes through the North and South poles of the planet. This line is called the *axis of rotation*. Earth rotates from west to east around this axis once every 24 hours. During this period, sunlight and darkness fall across all oceans, nations, and peoples, with morning and evening occurring at opposite sides of Earth's sphere. This project attempts to re-create the light and shadowed areas of Earth for a given time of day using a model globe and compass.

## Procedure

A model globe is placed outside and oriented so that its North Pole points to Earth's magnetic north. The globe is turned so that the observer's location is at the top.

## Hypothesis

The globe will show the actual illuminated and shadowed parts of Earth at the time the observation is made.

## Experiment to Test Hypothesis

**1.** Find a globe that can be detached from its base. Take the globe outside into direct sunlight, preferably near a telephone pole, flagpole, or similar object.

**2.** Place the glass jar on a flat surface and position the globe in the mouth of the jar.

**3.** Rotate the globe until your location on Earth appears at the top center of the globe.

**4.** Use the compass to find north. While keeping your location at the top center, rotate the globe until its North Pole points in the direction of due north, as indicated by the compass.

**5.** Put a tiny glob of clay over your location at the top of the globe. Stick a toothpick in the clay and notice the direction and length of its shadow. Now look up at the telephone pole near you. What do you see?

## Results & Conclusions

We set up our globe at 1:00 P.M. in the parking lot of a supermarket. The parking lot was ideal because it was wide, sunny, and contained several high lampposts with clearly visible shadows. Comparing lamppost to toothpick shadows gave us the first clue that the illuminated part of the globe was the same as the illuminated part of Earth. The ratio of lamppost shadow to actual lamppost was the same as the ratio of toothpick shadow to actual toothpick—each shadow about one-third the length of the physical object. This meant that the globe and Earth were precisely aligned for that particular time of day and that the globe's axis of rotation was parallel to Earth's axis of rotation.

After about 15 minutes, the temperatures on the globe varied, with the warmest area occurring in the *subsolar point* directly in line between the sun and the center of the globe. (The subsolar point is always within 23.5° of the equator.) As is true on the actual Earth, areas surrounding the subsolar point show progressive cooling until the poles, where the glancing sunlight produces hardly any warmth at all. Finally, since our observation occurred in February, the southern pole was in sunlight while the northern pole was in shadow—the full picture of Earth's hours, temperatures, and seasons in miniature!

# Eight

# PHYSICS *Surprises*

# Bubbles & Antibubbles

*Is it possible to create antibubbles in a solution of distilled water, detergent, and salt?*

## Materials
- clear drinking glass
- small bowl
- teaspoon
- distilled water
- clear dishwashing detergent
- table salt
- 6 inches (15 cm) thin copper wire
- ear-bulb-style squeezer

## Background
Antibubbles are interesting to physicists because they teach about the elastic and attractive properties of water. An antibubble is the opposite of a normal bubble. A typical soap bubble consists of a film of water surrounding a pocket of air. But an antibubble is made when a thin layer of air surrounds a liquid. Normal bubbles have air inside and outside (soap bubbles in air) or inside only (air bubbles in water). But an antibubble will always have water inside and a layer of air containing the water.

Antibubbles form when a droplet falls quickly into a very clean body of water. The droplet presses through the water's surface with a thin wrapping of air. This wrap coats the bubble but isn't buoyant enough to cause the bubble to float to the surface. This is why antibubbles can have a strange,
weightless quality. Another difference between normal bubbles and antibubbles is the way they pop. When a soap bubble pops, it leaves behind a tiny droplet of soap. When an antibubble pops, it leaves behind a tiny bubble—the remains of the film of air that covered it.

## Procedure
An antibubble solution is made with distilled water, detergent, and a little salt. The solution is poured into a clear glass, and a bubble-making squeezer (made from a rubber ear-bulb) is used to create the antibubbles.

## Hypothesis
The procedure, though delicate, will successfully create antibubbles in the glass. The bubbles will be observed floating and popping.

## Experiment to Test Hypothesis
**1.** Place 1 teaspoon (5 ml) of liquid detergent and a pinch of salt into the bottom of an empty glass. Fill the glass almost to the top with distilled water. Stir the water until the soap and salt disappear, and then allow the water to stand overnight to release any gases.

**2.** Place the glass in the bowl and continue to fill the glass with more distilled water until it begins to overflow into the bowl. The overflow "sweeps" the surface of the water clean and keeps any debris from popping your bubble.

**3.** Wrap one end of the copper wire around the narrow part of the ear bulb and extend the other end out about 2 inches (5 cm), bending it down so that it makes contact with the water. The copper wire will act as a ground to keep static electricity from breaking your antibubbles.

**4.** Squeeze the bulb, place the tip in the overflow water, and release your grip so that the bulb fills with water.

**5.** To make the first antibubble, hold the tip of the bulb about ¼ inch (0.635 cm) from the surface of the glass so that the tip of the copper wire makes contact with the water. Give the bulb a short, strong squeeze.

**6.** Replenish the bulb with more overflow water and repeat the previous step. Observe your results.

**7.** After you've created a few good-size, healthy antibubbles in the glass, poke one of them with the end of the copper wire and watch what happens.

**Results & Conclusions**

Although the first five attempts at creating antibubbles were not successful, a ¼-inch-size (about 0.635 cm) bubble finally resulted from the sixth squeeze of the bulb. Unlike an ordinary air bubble, the antibubble looked almost jewellike and had a pearly iridescence. It also behaved unusually because it hovered just below the surface of the water and didn't show a tendency to either float up or sink down.

Popping the antibubble produced, as expected, a tiny bubble—about one-tenth the size of the antibubble—composed entirely from the layer of air surrounding the original antibubble. This bubble did what most ordinary bubbles do: It rose quickly to the top.

# Conserve Heat in a Swimming Pool

*Does planting foliage around a swimming pool conserve water heat?*

## Materials

- shallow wash basin (or similar container)
- electric fan
- stack of books
- outdoor thermometer
- clock with second hand
- tape
- 5 small potted geraniums or similar broad-leaf plants
- warm water
- pitcher
- adult helper

**Caution:** *This project requires that you place an electrical appliance close to water, so adult help is required. Do not bring the fan into contact with the water, and make sure that your hands are dry whenever you touch the fan.*

## Background

Although most people prefer to swim in heated pools, keeping a pool warm can be very expensive. When a pool is warmer than the surrounding air temperature, heat radiates from the surface of the pool and is lost. Wind blowing across the surface of the pool accelerates this loss up to 50%. Many people place chain-link or iron-bar fences around their pools as a safety feature. However, these fence designs do little to affect the loss of heat from the pool's surface.

## Procedure

A shallow basin is filled with warm water and a base temperature taken. A fan is positioned so that it blows across the surface of the water, and the drop in water temperature is noted over a period of time. We repeat the procedure, but this time with a row of plants placed along the side of the basin.

## Hypothesis

The row of plants will allow the water to retain heat for a longer period of time.

## Experiment to Test Hypothesis

**1.** Place the basin on a flat surface and build up one side with books so that you have a platform even with the basin's top edge.

**2.** Tape the thermometer to an inside wall of the basin.

**3.** Position the electric fan so that it blows across the top of the basin. Test it out, but switch off the fan; you'll need it a little later.

**4.** Turn on the hot water tap and allow the water to run for about 60 seconds. Fill a pitcher with water and add the water to the basin until it's almost level with the top.

**5.** Watch the thermometer. You want the temperature to stabilize at 100° Fahrenheit (37.8° Centigrade). If the water is too hot, wait until it cools. If the water is too cool, run the tap until you get very hot water and add it to the basin.

**6.** At 100° F (37.8° C), look at your clock and note the time. Then turn on the electric fan and watch the thermometer. Determine how long it takes for the water to cool 5° F (2.8° C). When you've got your reading, empty the basin.

**7.** Place a row of potted plants on the books so that they break the stream of the electric fan. Then repeat Steps 4 through 6. Record and compare temperature readings.

**Results & Conclusions**

Adding a row of plants to the basin setup allowed the water to stay warm longer. In fact, while the unprotected pool cooled 5° F (about 2.8° C) in only 3 minutes, the protected pool took nearly twice that long to cool. This project suggests that by adding a windbreaker in the form of plant foliage, the surface cooling of water by the action of wind can be drastically reduced. This means that a heated pool stays warm longer when surrounded by high bushes. It also means a smaller pool heating bill.

# Winterize a Swimming Pool

*Is it a good idea to drain a swimming pool in the winter?*

## Materials

- four 24-fluid-ounce (720-ml) disposable rectangular food-storage containers
- 2 shallow plastic basins (at least 2x wider than food-storage containers)
- plaster of Paris
- petroleum jelly or vegetable shortening
- rubber cement
- fine sandpaper
- turquoise spray paint
- 2 heavy books
- soil (to fill one basin; from backyard or schoolyard)
- watering can with sprinkler head
- water

## Background

Many people believe that it's necessary to drain a swimming pool in the winter. This is because, at freezing temperatures, the water freezes and the expansion of ice against the pool walls might crack the concrete. Since it's true that ice takes up more space than liquid water, draining a pool during the winter months seems like a good idea. This is supported by the fact that most outdoor pools in recreation centers, parks, and country clubs appear to be emptied during winter.

## Procedure

Two model swimming pool shells are made from plaster. Each shell is placed in the center of a shallow basin and surrounded with soil. Pool 1 is filled with water and Pool 2 remains dry. The soil around each pool is completely saturated with water (to simulate wet winter weather) and both basins are put in the freezer. After 24 hours, the basins are removed and the pools inspected for damage.

## Hypothesis

The empty pool will show no damage while the filled pool will show cracking.

## Experiment to Test Hypothesis

**1.** Use petroleum jelly to coat the insides of two plastic food-storage containers. Label the containers #1 and #2.

**2.** In a separate bowl, mix enough plaster to completely fill one of the containers. Pour this plaster into container #1 to about the halfway mark.

**3.** Take another container and insert it, round side down, into container #1. Push down until the plaster is forced up the walls of container #1 and begins to seep out the top. Place a heavy book on the joined containers and leave them undisturbed for at least 24 hours.

**4.** Repeat the previous step for container #2. After 24 hours, carefully pull the container pairs apart, and you should have two perfectly formed swimming pool shells. Wipe any residual petroleum jelly off, sandpaper irregularities you see on the edges or surfaces, and then paint the inside of each shell turquoise. Finally, coat the outside of each pool with rubber cement.

**5.** Fill both basins with soil to a depth equal to the depth of the swimming pools. Insert a pool into the center of each basin, hollowing out soil where necessary. Pat the soil down so that it's firm around the pools. Label the basins Pool 1 and Pool 2.

**6.** Add water to Pool 1 so that it's about three-quarters full. Leave Pool 2 dry.

**7.** Fill the watering can and sprinkle water on the soil surrounding both pools. Stop when the soil is very wet.

**8.** If you have enough room, place both basins in the freezer and leave them for about 24 hours. If there's room for only one basin, do them one at a time, but have a camera ready to record the results.

**9.** Remove the basins and examine the pools. Allow the basins to thaw at room temperature for about 1 hour; then carefully remove the pools from the soil, flipping them upside down. Make additional observations and compare results.

**Results & Conclusions**

Despite what we might read, hear, or even see, the results of this project warned that it's not a good idea to drain a swimming pool in the winter. In soil, the expansion of water into ice exerts considerable force on the unsupported walls of an underground pool. Without an equal counterforce applied to the soil, the walls of an empty pool will crack. Keeping a pool filled in the winter provides the counterforce needed to minimize the surrounding pressure of ice.

When Pool 1 was removed from the freezer, the pool water was indeed frozen, as was the soil surrounding the pool, but the pool shell appeared intact. This was confirmed by pulling the pool out of the soil and flipping it over. There were no cracks in the plaster at all.

When Pool 2 was removed from the freezer, it was immediately apparent that the pressure from the surrounding frozen soil had cracked the plaster shell in several places. The cracks were most conspicuous along the long walls of the shell. It was very difficult to pull this shell out of the soil—the rubber cement barely held it together—but flipping it over showed the seriousness of the cracks. This project shows that keeping a pool filled in the winter protects it against ice damage. Keeping water in the pool equalizes pressure and provides additional structural support when the surrounding ground freezes, expands, and pushes against the pool walls.

# Fractured Cookie Dough

*Can we reproduce important geological events like tension fractures in cookie dough?*

## Materials
- mixing spoon
- large bowl
- measuring cup
- measuring spoons
- ¼x¼-inch x 2-foot (0.63x0.63x60-cm) square dowels
- wooden cutting board (or similar smooth surface)
- rolling pin
- knife

## Cookie Dough Recipe
- ¼ pound (115 g) butter (softenedat room temperature)
- ¾ cup (150 g) sugar
- 1 egg
- ½ teaspoon (2.5 ml) vanilla
- 1 tablespoon (15 ml) cream or milk
- 1¼ cups (175 g) flour
- ⅛ teaspoon (0.31 ml or pinch) salt
- ¼ teaspoon (1.25 ml) baking powder

## Background
Big faults can be bad news for the people living in earthquake-prone areas. The faults, also known as *tension fractures*, can appear as deep cracks on glaciers, or as the magma-filled dikes that supply molten rock to the "curtain of fire" eruptions in Hawaii. A more everyday example is cracks in the surface of an asphalt road. Tension fractures form because the crust of Earth gets pulled and stretched by the motion of the huge plates that continually slide around and beneath each other. These *tectonic forces* create the fractures, some of which will link together to form larger faults.

## Procedure
The cookie dough is rolled into a thin flat sheet, sliced in various places, and then slowly pulled apart to observe the creation and spread of tension fractures. (When the experiment is completed, the cookie dough can be baked into cookies!)

## Hypothesis
The fractures will have a similar look to those seen on an asphalt road.

## Experiment to Test Hypothesis

**1.** Mix the cookie dough in a bowl. (By hand, first mix the butter and sugar. Add the egg, vanilla, and milk, and mix. Then sift the flour with the salt and baking powder. Slowly add the flour mixture to the butter-sugar-egg, etc., mixture.)

**2.** Spread an even layer of flour on the cutting board.

**3.** Place the dough on the board and smooth it out with the rolling pin. Add more flour to the cutting board to keep the dough from sticking.

**4.** When the layer of dough is about ¼ inch (0.63 cm) thick, cut away the edges to make a square with 8-inch (20.32-cm) sides.

**5.** Carefully lift the dough square and spread some more flour underneath. The square must slide easily for the project to work.

**6.** Place the wooden dowels over the left and right edge of the square. You will use these dowels to apply uniform pressure when pulling the dough apart.

**7.** Placing your hands on the dowels, slowly stretch the cookie dough and observe what happens.

**8.** Roll the dough into another sheet and trim as before.

**9.** Use the knife to make an inch-long (2.54-cm) incision in the middle of the dough square, parallel to the sides of the square.

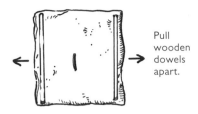

Cookie Dough Squared
1-inch incision in middle

Slowly stretch the dough again, observing the result. When you're finished, roll the dough into another sheet.

**10.** Make two incisions near the middle of the dough, about 2 inches (5 cm) apart, and offset them diagonally from each other.

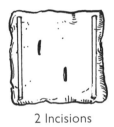

2 Incisions

Stretch the dough again, observing the result. When you're finished, roll the dough into another sheet.

**11.** Try making a stair-step pattern of incisions. Make up your own patterns and see how they deform when you stretch the dough.

Stair-Step Pattern of Incisions

## Results & Conclusions

Stretching the uncut dough created tears in the dough at the edges where the dowels pressed down. The tears appeared random and unrelated to any features in the dough itself.

After the first incision was made, stretching the dough concentrated the tearing around the incision, which now became a propagating fracture. The tearing proceeded from the pointed tips of the incision and moved faster as the incision widened.

After the two-stepped incisions were made, stretching the dough concentrated the tearing around the pointed tips as before. But this time, as the fractures from each incision moved past each other, they turned inward and joined together, forming one large fracture.

From these observations, we can conclude that as the dough was stretched, tensional stress was created throughout the volume of dough. The incisions created a "defect" because the stress cannot be transmitted across the defect (the walls of the incision can't pull on each other). So stress that would ordinarily be transmitted across the defect is instead concentrated at the edges of the defect. The bigger the fracture gets, the more stress concentrates at the tip of the fracture.

This is why it gets easier to stretch the dough as the fracture grows. When the tips of two fractures begin to pass each other, the direction of tensional stress changes because the stress cannot be transmitted in a straight line across that gap. This means that the stress is curved around by both of the fracture tips. Every new pattern of incisions made demonstrated this principle of fractures concentrating at the tips of incisions and eventually joining each other.

Our hypothesis was correct in that the resulting fracture patterns in cookie dough resembled the texture of an asphalt road that has been stressed and fractured as a result of tectonic motions.

# Gelatin Refraction

*How does the refraction of light differ between gelatin and water?*

## Materials
- piece of white paper
- marking pen
- unflavored gelatin mix
- petri dish
- glass
- ¼-teaspoon (1.25-ml) measuring spoon
- hot water

## Background
In physics, the law of reflection states that light will always reflect at an angle identical to the angle of its source. But one of light's many unusual properties is that it can be bent, or refracted, when it passes through various substances. For example, if you place a pencil in a glass of water, the top (dry) half of the pencil seems disconnected from the submerged half of the pencil.

This is because light travels faster through air than through water, so it bends slightly when passing from one medium to another. In general, the denser the medium, the greater the resulting refraction. So, when it comes to refraction, air is to water as water is to a denser substance, like gelatin, as we'll see.

## Procedure
A special lens is made from gelatin and the petri dish. The word "hello" is read, first through the gelatin lens, and then after water is added to the lens.

## Hypothesis
The written word "hello" will be readable through both the gelatin and the water.

## Experiment to Test Hypothesis
**1.** Place the petri dish on a sheet of white paper and trace the outline of the dish on the paper. Remove the dish and write "hello" in the circle you traced. Replace the petri dish so that the word appears clearly through the bottom of the dish.

**2.** Mix the unflavored gelatin with hot water and allow it to cool. Place a few spoonfuls of gelatin in a glass and chop it into gravel-size chunks.

**3.** Spoon the chunks into the petri dish so that they just cover the bottom. Can you still recognize the word "hello" underneath?

**4.** Pour enough water into the dish to just cover the gelatin chunks. Can you read the word now?

### Results & Conclusions

The hypothesis was incorrect in that there was a distinct difference between the clarity of the word "hello" when viewed through the gelatin than when viewed through the water. Although gelatin is mostly water, its slightly greater density resulted in a steeper angle of refraction as the light passed through it. Because the gelatin was broken into chunks, the light was scattered twice, once by the uneven sides of the gelatin pieces going in, and a second time on the way out. Light, highly refracted and scattered in all different directions, made the word "hello" impossible to read. But when water was added to the gelatin, the light passed through both gelatin and water without bending and so was reflected—rather than refracted—back to our eyes.

# Half-Full or Half-Empty?

*If you fill two identical glasses with fine gravel and pebbles, does each glass have the same amount of empty space between particles?*

## Materials
- 2 tall glasses (same size)
- measuring cup (with milliliters)
- aquarium gravel
- pebbles
- strainer
- bowl

## Background
By measuring the empty space, or *pore volume*, of a given substance, scientists can determine how much liquid it will contain. This kind of information is very useful when studying the effect liquid will have on soil, sand, rocks, and other types of materials. For example, scientists know that it's much more difficult to extract crude oil from materials with a low pore volume, such as sand, than from materials with a higher pore volume, such as rocky soil. Understanding pore volume also helps scientists determine patterns of erosion and the stability of surfaces when exposed to water. For example, the addition of water to a certain type of sand results in the liquefaction of the sand into "quicksand," sticky enough to swallow a beach house!

## Procedure
We fill two identical glasses with gravel and pebbles, add water, and compare the amount of empty space between the two glasses by pouring off and measuring the volume of water.

## Hypothesis
The gravel and pebbles should have the same amount of pore volume. The different sizes of each "particle" should not affect the amount of space between them.

## Experiment to Test Hypothesis
**1.** Pour gravel into a tall glass to the rim.

**2.** Pour the gravel from the glass into a measuring cup and record the gravel volume in milliliters (550 ml).

**3.** Pour the gravel back into the glass and pour water into the glass until it covers the gravel and creates a *meniscus* (bulge) at the rim of the glass.

**4.** Strain the water from the glass into a bowl.

**5.** Pour the water from the bowl into a measuring cup and note the pore volume in milliliters (250 ml).

**6.** Divide the pore volume (250 ml) by the gravel volume (550 ml) for an answer of 0.45.

**7.** Multiply 0.45 by 100 to find the total percentage of pore volume (45%) for 550 ml of gravel. This means that the glass of gravel is 45% empty space!

**8.** Repeat Steps 1 through 5 with the pebbles, noting that the pore volume for the pebbles is 300 milliliters.

**9.** Divide the pore volume (300 ml) by the gravel volume (550 ml) for an answer of 0.54.

**10.** Multiply 0.54 by 100 to find the total percentage of pore volume (54%) for 550 ml of pebbles. This means that the glass of pebbles is 54% empty space!

## Results & Conclusions

Our hypothesis was incorrect. Both times the experiment was performed, there was about 9% more pore volume for the pebbles than for the gravel. Since the pebbles were larger than the gravel, there was more pore space left between them for the water to fill. Also, because the gravel was smaller, it packed more closely together and began to resemble a semipermeable solid. In simpler terms, the glass of gravel was slightly more than half-full, while the glass of pebbles was slightly more than half-empty!

# Non-Newtonian Two-Step

*Using simple materials, is it possible to demonstrate the properties of Newtonian and non-Newtonian fluids?*

## Materials
- box of cornstarch
- large bowl
- 2 shallow shirt boxes with covers
- 2 plastic trash bags
- paper clips
- newspaper
- old pair of shoes

## Background
The study of moving fluids is called *rheology*, and rheologists classify fluid mechanics into two basic types: Newtonian and non-Newtonian. Of the two types, Newtonian fluids have a constant flow rate, or *viscosity*, at a given temperature. Water is an example of a Newtonian fluid. But a mixture of cornstarch and water is non-Newtonian because it has a variable flow rate at a given temperature. In fact, as this project demonstrates, pressure has a lot to do with how a cornstarch and water mixture behaves.

## Procedure
Four box halves are filled with a cornstarch and water mixture. The boxes are walked on to see if pressure affects the viscosity of the mixture—one of the properties of a non-Newtonian fluid.

## Hypothesis
The weight of each footstep will harden the cornstarch so that none of it sticks to our shoes.

## Experiment to Test Hypothesis
**1.** Place newspapers over a section of floor where you intend to do the project.

**2.** Remove the covers from the shirt boxes and place them open side up.

**3.** Cut apart two plastic trash bags and line the two boxes and two covers with plastic. Use paper clips to attach the plastic to the edges of the boxes if necessary.

**4.** Place the boxes and covers in a stepping-stone arrangement so that you can easily walk across them without touching the floor in between.

**5.** Stir the cornstarch and water in the bowl until you have a puttylike substance, adding a little more cornstarch or water if necessary.

**6.** Divide the cornstarch and water mixture equally between the boxes and covers and allow the mixture to settle.

**7.** Stand behind the first box in the row and begin stepping across, placing your feet directly on each box. See if you can step across without getting any of the cornstarch and water solution on your feet.

### Results & Conclusions

Stepping fast meant keeping our feet dry. Slow two-steppers sank into the cornstarch and water mixture and gooped up their shoes. It was clear that the harder and faster we walked, the firmer the mixture became. A pause of only a few seconds resulted in a slow sink.

Our two-stepping showed that pressure affected the viscosity of the cornstarch and water mixture (more pressure, more viscosity) and so the mixture was a non-Newtonian fluid.

But to understand why, we had to learn a little more about cornstarch and what actually happens to it when it's added to water.

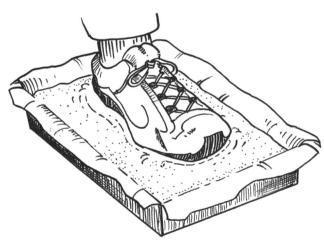

For one thing, cornstarch doesn't really dissolve. And yet each particle of dissolved starch is too small to see or easily filter out of the water. Scientists call this arrangement a *colloid,* because the particles are larger than molecules but small enough to remain suspended in the liquid indefinitely. In the case of cornstarch, the particles are of two kinds—crystalline and noncrystalline. The noncrystalline particles are spongelike and absorb water, while the crystalline particles do not absorb water.

When we applied pressure to the cornstarch mixture, we crushed the crystals into smaller particles that could also absorb water. This meant that crushing made the mixture "drier," at least while the pressure was on. As soon as we relaxed the pressure, the crystals re-formed again, releasing their water, and the mixture became wet.

If a stepper paused too long, the initial impact of the step was absorbed by the starch and carried away from the point of contact. This allowed the cornstarch to soften again in regions close to the foot and firm up in areas farther away. The result? A sinking stepper.

# Raisins Versus Popcorn Buoyancy Test

*Will raisins and popcorn kernels show different degrees of buoyancy when placed in clear water or carbonated water?*

## Materials
- glass of clear water
- glass of seltzer (carbonated water)
- raisins
- unpopped popcorn kernels

## Background
For an object to float, it must displace—or push aside—an amount of water equal to the weight of the object itself. The hull of a boat is perfectly designed to do this since the wide curved surface of the hull displaces water efficiently, supporting the boat's weight. But how about objects like raisins and corn kernels? Although each contains a small amount of interior air and enough skin texture to hold surface bubbles, neither the raisin nor the kernel displaces enough water to remain afloat. Still, both objects have special surface features that come into play when the medium is carbonated, not ordinary, water, as this project will demonstrate.

## Procedure
Several raisins are dropped into a glass of plain water, followed by several popcorn kernels. Raisins and kernels are dropped into a second glass of carbonated water and the results compared.

## Hypothesis
Both raisins and kernels will sink to the bottom of the glass containing plain water. In the carbonated water, the wrinkled skin of the raisin will allow carbonation bubbles to stick until the raisin floats to the surface. However, the smooth-skinned popcorn kernel will remain at the bottom.

## Experiment to Test Hypothesis
1. Fill one glass with ordinary water and a second glass with carbonated water.

2. Drop three raisins in the first, ordinary water glass and observe what happens. Follow with three popcorn kernels.

3. Drop three raisins into the second, carbonated water glass and watch them. Follow with three popcorn kernels.

4. Compare how the raisins and kernels behave in the two glasses of water.

## Results & Conclusions

Raisins and kernels sank to the bottom of the glass containing plain water. After a few minutes, some bubbles appeared on their surfaces, but the bubbles were too small and too few to bring any of the raisins or kernels back to the surface. When raisins and kernels were dropped into the carbonated water, they too sank to the bottom. But after only 20 seconds, a thick coating of bubbles appeared—first on the raisins and then on the kernels. After about a minute, each raisin—covered with bubbles—floated to the surface and remained there. The kernels followed, also covered with bubbles. This meant that the hypothesis was only half correct since it didn't seem that the surface texture of the kernels would be rough enough to keep the bubbles attached.

The mechanics of carbonated buoyancy works this way: Carbonated water contains carbon dioxide gas ($CO_2$) which, although heavier than ordinary air, is still lighter than water. This is why the $CO_2$ bubbles fizzle to the top in soda water. Capillary action attracts the $CO_2$ to the surface of both raisin and kernel. Here the gassy bubbles stick, accumulate, and combine. Soon each raisin and kernel is surrounded by a bubble overcoat of $CO_2$ that floats to the surface. The bubbles find nicks and rough spots on the raisin and kernel surfaces and stick there. Apparently, from the $CO_2$ bubble's point of view, the surface of a popcorn kernel is no smoother than the wrinkled skin of a raisin.

# Sky in a Bottle

*Is it possible to simulate the sky's scattering of blue and red light in a medium made up of milky water?*

## Materials
- large jar with straight sides (super-size jellybean jar)
- 3 cups (720 ml) whole milk
- tea bag
- flashlight (Mini Maglite)

## Background
The blue sky above us results from what physicists call a selective scattering of light. When white sunlight—actually a mix of all colors—passes through Earth's atmosphere, molecules of air, water, and particles of dust absorb most of the colors but reflect and scatter the rest. Smaller particles scatter shorter wavelengths (blue light) and larger particles scatter longer wavelengths (red light). Blue light bounces in all directions and seems to fill the air with blue color. Red light is scattered less and tends to pass through the atmosphere in one direction only.

A deep blue sky means not only that the particles in our atmosphere are very small, but also that the air is relatively free of dust, water vapor, or man-made pollutants. Impurities in the air will "wash out" the deepest hues of the sky and turn it a whitish brown or gray.

The scattering of light can be simulated by using a suspension of whole milk in water. The particles of fat and protein in milk disperse in uniform particles, which will allow for a scattering very similar to that of the atmosphere. Polluting the milky water with other liquids will wash out the scattering of blue light and produce a "smoggy sky."

## Procedure
Milk is added to a large jar of clear water to make it slightly cloudy. We hold a flashlight against the jar in various positions to simulate the scattering of light through suspended particles. A tea bag is added to the water and its effect observed.

## Hypothesis
The milky water will display the familiar colors and light-scattering properties of the sky. The tea bag will make those properties harder to recognize.

## Experiment to Test Hypothesis
1. Fill the jar three-quarters full with water and add 3 cups (720 ml) of whole milk. Stir until the water has a uniform cloudiness.

**2.** Darken the room and point the flashlight down through the top edge of the jar so that the beam enters the water from the top surface. Observe the jar from the side.

**3.** Place the flashlight against the side of the jar and observe again.

**4.** Place the flashlight opposite you so that you look through the jar and directly into the beam of the flashlight.

**5.** Add a tea bag to the milky water, allow it to steep a few minutes, then stir the water and repeat Steps 1 through 4.

### Results & Conclusions

The hypothesis was correct. When the flashlight beam entered the water at an angle from above, the water seemed iridescent with a light blue color. The beam, also bluish, could be seen slicing through the water. When the beam was held against the jar's side, the blue appeared again although it was less intense. This paler blue was probably due to the fact that the light traveled a shorter distance sideways through the water and didn't scatter as much.

When the beam was looked at directly through the jar, it was reddish in color—almost like a setting sun. This was because, as explained, red light passes through the particles and is scattered less by them. Adding a tea bag to the milky water removed these scattering effects. In fact, not only did the bluish or reddish tint disappear when the flashlight was held in its familiar positions, but the beam itself was less distinct. The contaminants of the tea bag represented pollution and how it can remove the pure colors of the sky.

# Nine

# AMUSING *Math*

# A Different Shape for Dice

*Adult Help Required*

*Besides the cube, which polyhedrons can be used for dice?*

## Materials

- heavy cardstock
- photocopier (machine) that enlarges
- metal ruler
- craft knife
- scissors
- cellophane tape
- marking pen
- adult helper

**Caution:** *This project requires using a craft knife. Adult help is required.*

## Background

In geometry, a polyhedron is defined as any solid formed by plane faces. A cube is a simple polyhedron of six faces. It's no surprise then that a cube is the preferred shape for a die, since each of its six faces has an equal chance of turning up after a throw.

Mathematicians say a geometric object is "fair" when each face of the object has the same relationship with all other faces of the object, and each face of the object has the same relationship with the center of gravity. This means that polyhedrons other than a cube can be used for dice, even though many of them are quite complex geometrically.

In the mid-18th century, the Swiss mathematician Leonhard Euler came up with a formula that tested any polyhedron for fairness. *Euler's rule* states that when the number of a polyhedron's edges is subtracted from the sum of its faces and vertices (corners), the result must be 2. For example, a cube has 6 faces, 8 vertices, and 12 edges. A simple arithmetic calculation yields the number 2, just as Euler predicted. As far as polyhedrons go, the cube is fair.

Using Euler's rule and a basic understanding of fairness in polyhedrons, it's possible to construct polyhedrons of increasing complexity, test them with Euler's rule, and then throw them to record the number patterns that result.

**Note:** *Although looking for corners is the best way to recognize vertices, in geometry a vertex is defined as the point opposite to and farthest from the base of a figure.*

## Procedure

Four polyhedrons are constructed—cube, octahedron, pentagonal dipyramid, and dodecahedron—and each face numbered. The polyhedrons are first tested for fairness by Euler's rule, then thrown 100 times so that their number patterns can be compared.

## Hypothesis

Although the more complex polyhedrons will have more sides and therefore more numbers, each number should appear with the same frequency for every polyhedron.

## Experiment to Test Hypothesis

**1.** Enlarge the following patterns onto a piece of cardstock and cut them out around the edges. The dark lines should be lightly scored with a craft knife and ruler and then folded in one direction. Tape the edges to keep the polyhedrons together.

**2.** Write the numbers 1 through 6 on the faces of the cube.

Write the numbers 1 through 8 on the faces of the octahedron.

Write the numbers 1 through 10 on the faces of the pentagonal dipyramid.

Write the numbers 1–12 on the faces of the dodecahedron.

**3.** Apply Euler's rule to each polyhedron. Add the number of faces to the number of vertices and subtract the number of edges. Is each polyhedron fair?

**4.** Throw the cube die 100 times and record how many times each number appears. Repeat this procedure for the remaining polyhedrons, listing how many times each number appears in a table.

CUBE (6 sides)—object (left) and pattern (right).

OCTAHEDRON (8 sides)—object (left) and pattern (right).

PENTAGONAL DIPYRAMID (10 sides)—object (left) and pattern (right).

DODECAHEDRON (12 sides)—object (left) and pattern (right).

## Results & Conclusions

As expected, each polyhedron conformed to Euler's rule by providing a remainder of 2 after the appropriate addition and subtraction was performed.

Mathematically at least, the polyhedrons were fair. In the real world, this fairness was supported by throwing each polyhedron 100 times and recording number frequency. The results are shown in the tables on the next page.

For 100 throws, each numbered face on the cube appeared an average of 16.7 times. This meant that the total for each number represented approximately one-sixth of the total throws, a distribution pattern that supported the cube's fairness.

## Cube (100 throws)

| Face Number | Frequency |
| --- | --- |
| 1 | 15 |
| 2 | 18 |
| 3 | 16 |
| 4 | 19 |
| 5 | 17 |
| 6 | 15 |

## Octahedron

| Face Number | Frequency |
| --- | --- |
| 1 | 12 |
| 2 | 13 |
| 3 | 14 |
| 4 | 13 |
| 5 | 11 |
| 6 | 10 |
| 7 | 12 |
| 8 | 15 |

## Pentagonal Dipyramid

| Face Number | Frequency |
| --- | --- |
| 1 | 9 |
| 2 | 10 |
| 3 | 11 |
| 4 | 8 |
| 5 | 10 |
| 6 | 11 |
| 7 | 12 |
| 8 | 8 |
| 9 | 10 |
| 10 | 11 |

## Dodecahedron

| Face Number | Frequency |
| --- | --- |
| 1 | 9 |
| 2 | 9 |
| 3 | 8 |
| 4 | 7 |
| 5 | 8 |
| 6 | 9 |
| 7 | 10 |
| 8 | 9 |
| 9 | 8 |
| 10 | 7 |
| 11 | 8 |
| 12 | 8 |

For 100 throws, each number face on the octahedron appeared an average of 12.5 times. This meant that the total for each number represented approximately one-eighth of the total throws, proving that the octahedron was fair.

For 100 throws, each number face on the pentagonal dipyramid appeared an average of 10 times. This meant that the total for each number represented approximately one-tenth of the total throws. The pentagonal dipyramid was fair.

For 100 throws, each number face on the dodecahedron appeared an average of 8.3 times. This meant that the total for each number represented approximately one-twelfth of the total throws, so the dodecahedron was fair.

The interesting implication of

Euler's rule is that even the most complex polyhedrons can work as dice, though a more complicated shape might roll around a bit before settling down.

Can a fair polyhedron with nonidentical faces or vertices exist? The question was partially answered by the pentagonal dipyramid. Although the faces of the pentagonal dipyramid were identical triangles, the solid form of it consisted of two pentagonal pyramids joined together at the bases. This meant that the pentagonal dipyramid had two vertices of 5 intersections and four vertices of 4 intersections. The pentagonal dipyramid was unlike any of the other polyhedrons in our group and yet it conformed to Euler's rule of fairness.

Take another solid form and you have a different story. For example, a classical pyramid with four triangular faces and one square face conforms to Euler's rule. But if the pyramid is short and fat, the square face will be landed upon more than a fifth of the time. If the pyramid is tall and thin, the square face will be landed upon less than a fifth of the time. Is there a height where the square face will be landed upon exactly one-fifth of the time? "Yes!" say the mathematicians. They tell us that if we knew the height, force, elasticity, and throwing method, the best dimension for the pyramid could be calculated. But once those conditions changed, the pyramid would no longer be fair.

# Calculate Bicycle-Gear Ratios

*Is it possible to calculate gear ratios on a 21-speed bicycle and then determine, for any gear combination, how much distance is covered for each pedal rotation?*

## Materials
- 21-speed bicycle (or 3-speed or 10-speed bicycle)
- white correction fluid
- tape measure
- calculator

## Background
The history of the bicycle goes back more than 500 years. Although sketches for a bicyclelike machine appear as early as 1490 in one of Leonardo da Vinci's notebooks, the inventor of the first true bicycle was the Frenchman Ernest Michaux. His velocipede of 1812 started a craze throughout Europe. But it was the British who introduced the bicycle as we know it today, a machine with pneumatic tires, ball bearings, wire-spoked wheels, and—most important of all—a variable-gear mechanism.

Variable gears make the bicycle one of the most efficient, and certainly the least polluting, means of transportation available. Multiple gears allow the bicyclist to select the appropriate gear ratio to match his or her power output to the slope and wind conditions.

This project will count gear teeth on a bicycle, calculate the ratios of the number of teeth on the front gear mechanism to the number of teeth on the rear gear mechanism, and then determine the distance covered for one wheel rotation in a given gear.

## Procedure
Pedal and wheel ratios are first "eyeballed" by rotating the pedal and wheel and comparing rotation rates. Then the number of teeth on each *gear ring* (at the rear of the bike) is divided into the number of teeth on each *gear cluster* (at the front of the bike) to obtain a set of gear ratios. Lower ratios are divided into higher ratios to obtain precise distances covered for each rotation of the pedal in a given gear.

## Hypothesis
The eyeballing will provide a rough estimate of the ratios. These will later be confirmed and refined by the calculations.

## Experiment to Test Hypothesis

**1.** Turn the bicycle upside down on the floor, balancing it on its handlebars and seat.

**2.** Hold a pedal and slowly rotate it clockwise. Notice how the rear wheel also rotates clockwise. Stop rotating the pedal and watch the wheel coast for a while; then hold your hand against the tire to brake the wheel.

**3.** Rotate the pedal again, but this time use the gear shift to change gears as the wheel is rotating. Notice how the chain connects one of the several circles of gear teeth in the front of the bicycle, called the *chain rings*, to one of many gears in the back, called the *cluster*.

**4.** Keep rotating the pedal and shift the bicycle into the lowest gear—the smallest front chain ring and the largest gear on the rear cluster. Stop rotating the pedal when the gears shift into place.

**5.** Position the pedal so that it's next to some part of the bicycle that will help you see when you've made a complete rotation.

**6.** Find the tire valve on the rear tire. Coast the rear wheel until the valve is straight up and down or next to some part of the bicycle where you can tell it's made a complete rotation.

**7.** Keeping your eye on both the pedal and wheel, rotate the pedal in one complete circle, and count the number of revolutions made by the rear wheel. Make sure you brake the wheel with your hand when you finish rotating the pedal. Write down this number. (If your wheel has 36 spokes, then you can more precisely estimate fractional parts of the rotation because each spoke is one-thirty-sixth of a circle or 10 degrees.)

**8.** Shift into high gear (the largest front chain ring and the smallest gear in the cluster) and repeat the previous step. Write down the number of total revolutions for the wheel.

**9.** To count the total number of teeth in the chain rings, place a dab of correction fluid on one tooth of each ring. Start with the largest ring and count around it, recording the number. Do the same for the remaining rings.

**10.** To count the total number of teeth in the gear cluster, place a dab of correction fluid on one tooth of each gear. Count around each gear and record the numbers.

**11.** To calculate gear ratios (how many times the bicycle wheel goes around for each complete rotation of the pedal), divide the number of teeth in each chain ring by the number of teeth in each cluster gear. Record the totals.

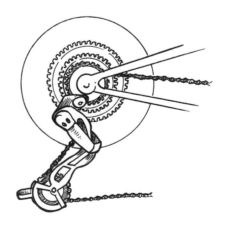

Calculate Bicycle-Gear Ratios **189**

| Cluster Gear | Number of Teeth | GEAR RATIO Chain Ring 1 (#teeth) divided by Cluster Gear Teeth | GEAR RATIO Chain Ring 1 (#teeth) divided by Cluster Gear Teeth | GEAR RATIO Chain Ring 1 (#teeth) divided by Cluster Gear Teeth |
|---|---|---|---|---|
| x | x | x | x | x |
| x | x | x | x | x |
| x | x | x | x | x |
| x | x | x | x | x |
| x | x | x | x | x |
| 3 | 22 | 1.27 | 1.72 | 2.18 |

**12.** Enter your data in a table resembling the one above. The table should have as many rows as your number of cluster gears and a column for each of your chain rings.

**13.** Referring to the data in your table, you can calculate the percentage of force required to move from each gear to the next higher one. Do this by dividing the higher chain gear ratio by the lower one.

**14.** To determine the distance the bicycle travels in one rotation of the pedal for any given gear, measure the circumference of the wheel with the tape measure, then multiply the circumference for each gear ratio.

### Results & Conclusions

In a bicycle, gear ratios determine how many times the rear bicycle wheel goes around for each complete rotation of a pedal. Cyclists use low gears for accelerating or going uphill, medium gears for maintaining constant speed, and high gears for downhill and downwind runs. The gears act like levers. A low gear converts the force exerted on the pedals into another slightly lesser force that acts over a slightly longer distance. A high gear converts pedal force into a much smaller force exerted over a much longer distance.

In a bicycle, as in a lever, work is *force multiplied by distance*. Energy remains the same through the system so that the force exerted on the pedals, times the distance the pedals move, equals the force exerted on the rim of the wheel, times the distance the wheel moves. This is the basic reason that bicycles are a very efficient means of transportation. The force applied by the tire to the road can be varied over a wide range while the force applied to the pedals remains constant.

The bicycle we used had three chain rings and seven cluster gears. The wheels each had 36 spokes and a circumference of 81 inches (206 cm). All of our arithmetic calculations were entered in the following table, which diagrams the 21 gear ratios, or "speeds" of our bike.

Going back to comparing pedal to wheel revolutions, when the smallest chain ring was attached to the largest gear on the gear cluster, the wheel rotated ⅚ (0.82) of the way for each complete rotation of the pedal. This was confirmed by the first figure in the third column. When the largest chain ring was attached to the smallest gear on the gear cluster, the result was 3⅖ (3.42) rotations of the wheel for each rotation of the pedal. This was confirmed by the last figure in the fifth column. The remaining gear ratios were calculated using arithmetic alone, following Step 11.

To calculate the percentage of force required to move from each gear to the next higher one, ratios were divided into each other. Following Step 13, we divided the higher ratio by the lower one. For example, for chain ring 1, we divided 1.16 by 0.82 for a ratio of 1.41. Next we divided 1.27 by 1.16 for a ratio of 1.09. Next we divided 1.40 by 1.27 for a ratio of 1.10, and continued dividing for the remaining ratios (1.10, 1.12, 1.14).

For a well-designed gear cluster, the ratio of one gear to the next is nearly constant across the cluster. The extra force required from your muscles goes up by the same percentage with each shift. For our cluster, each gear required an average of 14% more force.

Finally, we determined distance by multiplying the circumference of the wheel by gear ratios. Our 81-inch (205.74-cm) wheel multiplied by the highest gear ratio of 3.42 yielded the product 277. This meant that in the highest gear for our bicycle, each rotation of the pedal yielded 277 inches, or about 23 feet (704 cm). Using the same formula, we calculated that, in the lowest gear, each pedal rotation yielded about 5½ feet (165 cm). Bicyclists choose a low gear to climb hills, only going up a little on each pedal rotation, and choose a higher gear ratio on level ground.

| Cluster Gear | Number of Teeth | GEAR RATIO Chain Ring I (28 teeth) divided by Cluster Gear Teeth | GEAR RATIO Chain Ring I (38 teeth) divided by Cluster Gear Teeth | GEAR RATIO Chain Ring I (48 teeth) divided by Cluster Gear Teeth |
| --- | --- | --- | --- | --- |
| I | 34 | 0.82 (28 / 34 = 0.82) | 1.10 | 1.41 |
| 2 | 24 | 1.16 | 1.58 | 2.0 |
| 3 | 22 | 1.27 | 1.72 | 2.18 |
| 4 | 20 | 1.40 | 1.9 | 2.4 |
| 5 | 18 | 1.55 | 2.11 | 2.66 |
| 6 | 16 | 1.75 | 2.37 | 3.0 |
| 7 | 14 | 2.00 | 2.71 | 3.42 (48 / 14 = 3.42) |

# Fibonacci Model of Plant Growth

*Is it possible to construct a model plant that displays both the Fibonacci series and the Golden Ratio?*

## Materials

- circular protractor
- ruler
- 20-inch (50-cm) wooden dowel
- modeling clay
- 2 pieces cardstock paper
- green construction paper
- 7 green pipe cleaners
- 4 plastic drinking straws
- white liquid glue
- marking pen
- scissors
- hole punch
- calculator
- adult helper

## Background

In the year 1202, the mathematician Leonardo of Pisa—better known as Fibonacci—discovered that Nature contained an interesting mathematical secret. When certain processes of the natural world were examined closely enough, a numerical pattern underlying their organization became apparent. Fibonacci first recognized this numerical pattern through rabbit breeding. He noticed that a pair of rabbits, left alone in a contained space, would produce additional pairs in a unique numerical sequence.

These Fibonacci numbers, named in honor of their discoverer, are found everywhere in nature, but particularly in plants. Petals of flowers, seeds within fruits, and leaves on plants all show Fibonacci number groupings.

The rules behind Fibonacci numbers are quite simple: Each successive number is the sum of the previous two numbers.

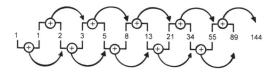

In mathematics, the Fibonacci numbers form a sequence defined recursively by:

$F_n$ = *the nth Fibonacci number*

To put it another way, you start with 0 and 1, and then produce the next Fibonacci number ($F_n$) by adding the two previous Fibonacci numbers:

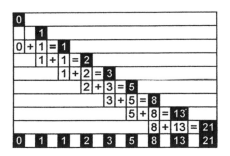

But the truly fascinating secret of the Fibonacci numbers—the one we'll explore in this project—is that the numbers relate to an important proportion found in Nature called the Golden Ratio, or *phi*.

First discovered by the Greeks, who named it after the sixteenth letter in their alphabet, the Golden Ratio describes the "ideal" properties of a length, object, or space. As such, the Ratio promises that something containing it will be aesthetically pleasing. Mathematically, the Golden Ratio is expressed as either $(1 - \sqrt{5}) \div 2 = -0.618$ or $(1 + \sqrt{5}) \div 2 = 1.618$. In practical terms, this means that—for any entity having the Golden Ratio—the relationship of the shorter side to the longer side is the same as the relationship of the longer side to the sum of the longer and shorter sides.

For example, if you draw a Golden Ratio rectangle 10 inches (25.4 cm) long and/or 6.18 inches (15.6 cm) wide, then divide it with a vertical line 6.18 inches from one end, you will have divided the rectangle into a square and a smaller rectangle. If you measure the proportions of the smaller rectangle, you'll find that it also has sides in the Golden Ratio. The small rectangle can therefore be subdivided in the same way indefinitely.

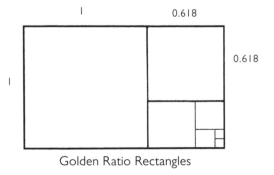

Golden Ratio Rectangles

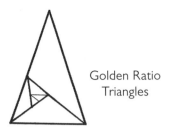

Golden Ratio Triangles

The Ratio can also be applied to other geometric shapes such as the triangle, and—as we'll see in this project—the circle. But for a circle to reflect the Golden Ratio, its proportional relationships must be applied to 360°. Here, as always, phi, in the form of 0.618, comes to the rescue. Phi allows us to divide the 360° of a circle into two arcs—one of which is 137.5°. This formula enables us to create a template for modeling our plant.

Mathematically, the Golden Ratio is an *irrational number*—neither a fraction nor a decimal—and can only be expressed approximately. But this "unmeasurable" quality of phi only adds to its mystery!

### Procedure
Using craft materials, a model plant is constructed with the help of a pie-shaped template containing the Golden Ratio.

### Hypothesis
The leaf arrangement of the model will display a structural similarity to leaf arrangements found in nature. Upon examination, this arrangement will reveal its usefulness to plants.

### Experiment to Test Hypothesis
1. Draw two circles, 6 inches (15.24 cm) in diameter. Cut them out.

**2.** Place the protractor over the first circle and carefully measure 137.5°, marking out a pie-shaped wedge in the circle.

**3.** Cut out the wedge. It represents the Golden Ratio applied to a circle.

**4.** Place the wedge over the second circle, then use the edge of the wedge to draw a line from the center of the circle to its rim. Label this line 1—it represents the first leaf of our plant.

**5.** Without moving the wedge, draw a line along its opposite side and label it 2—the second leaf of our plant.

**6.** Rotate the wedge so that the edge you used for line 1 is now against line 2. At the opposite side of the wedge, draw line 3—the third leaf. Keep rotating the wedge and drawing lines—representing leaves—until one of the lines overlaps a previous one. Count the total number of lines it took for this to happen.

**7.** Take the total number of lines and cut out as many leaves from the construction paper. The leaves should be philodendron shaped and graduated in length and width so that the smallest leaf is about 2x1 inches (5x2.54 cm) at the longest and widest part and the largest leaf is 7x3 inches (17.78x7.62 cm).

Leaf

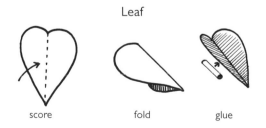

score        fold        glue

**8.** Cut the drinking straws into 13 pieces in graduated lengths from about 1 inch (2.54 cm) to 3 inches (7.62 cm) (size isn't crucial here). Glue the smallest length of straw vertically in the center of the smallest leaf and continue for all the leaves.

**9.** Stand the dowel upright in a lump of modeling clay or some other suitable base. Make sure you can easily walk completely around the dowel.

**10.** Punch a hole in the center of your lined circle and cut along one of the lines so you can open the circle and place it over the dowel. Slide the circle down to ½ inch (1.25 cm) from the bottom. Line 1 should face you.

**11.** Make a mark along the dowel at line 1. Without twisting the circle, move it up 1½ inches (3.81 cm) and mark the dowel at line 2. Continue moving the circle up in 1½-inch (3.81-cm) increments and marking the dowel at the numbered lines. You will create a spiral of marks leading to the top of the dowel. When you finish, slide the circle down the dowel to the base.

**12.** Cut the pipe cleaners into 6-inch (15-cm) lengths. At the bottom mark of the dowel, twist the first pipe cleaner. Look straight down at the circle and adjust the pipe cleaner to make sure it aligns with line 1. Twist another pipe cleaner at the next mark, and so on, until you've attached pipe cleaners to all marks on the dowel.

**13.** Starting from the bottom, slide the largest leaf onto the pipe cleaner. Slide the next largest leaf onto the next pipe cleaner, and so on, until all the leaves are attached to the dowel. Remember to look straight down while attaching leaves and use the Golden Ratio circle to guide you when necessary.

### Results & Conclusions

From rather primitive materials, we produced an unusually beautiful and lifelike plant. We attributed this to the fact that our model followed the mathematical rules of plant growth contained in the Fibonacci series and thus displayed the Golden Ratio.

Moving the 137.5° wedge around the circle, we found that we could draw 13 lines (a Fibonacci number representing a typical leaf arrangement about a stem) before line 14 overlapped line 1. In Nature, plants often grow spirals of leaves in clusters reflecting Fibonacci numbers.

The fact that the pattern eventually began to overlap itself says something important about the Golden Ratio. As mentioned, the value of phi is not a rational number, which means that it cannot be expressed exactly as a fraction or a decimal. Because of this, any Golden Ratio model we create—square, triangle, or circle—using conventional measurement tools will eventually become corrupted.

Still, the series of leaves attached to the spiral was pleasing to the eye, and looking at the model plant from directly above allowed us to appreciate Nature's architecture. Each of the plant's 13 leaves was fully exposed. If the sun were shining directly overhead, no leaf would be shadowed by a leaf above it. In this way, our model imitated the *primordia*, or growth tip, of a plant, which spirals upward and produces bracts for new leaves every 137.5°.

What remained was to show the relationship between the Golden Ratio and Fibonacci numbers, mentioned earlier. Here a calculator was necessary. To see the surprising connection between Fibonacci's amazing number discovery and the Golden Ratio celebrated by the ancient Greeks, we had to divide each Fibonacci number by the next higher number in the series.

$$1 / 1 = 1.000$$
$$1 / 2 = 0.500$$
$$2 / 3 = 0.666$$
$$3 / 5 = 0.600$$
$$5 / 8 = 0.625$$
$$8 / 13 = 0.615$$
$$13 / 21 = 0.619$$
$$21 / 34 = 0.617$$
$$34 / 55 = 0.618$$

Then we turned the procedure around and divided each Fibonacci number by the next lower number in the series.

$$55 / 34 = 1.618$$
$$34 / 21 = 1.619$$
$$21 / 13 = 1.615$$
$$13 / 8 = 1.625$$
$$8 / 5 = 1.600$$
$$5 / 3 = 1.666$$
$$3 / 2 = 1.500$$
$$2 / 1 = 2.000$$
$$1 / 1 = 1.000$$

The resulting lists showed that dividing adjacent Fibonacci numbers in either direction gradually approached decimal values of either 0.618 or 1.618—the Golden Ratio! From this you might say that Nature's wonders produce divine proportions, and divine proportions derive from Nature's wonders.

Our hypothesis was clearly supported. Better still, this project made it clear that both Fibonacci and the ancient Greeks saw beauty and mathematical order in the world around them.

# Fractals in Acrylic

*Can fractal patterns be created in the interface zone between acrylic paint and air?*

## Materials
- CD jewel case (discardable)
- black acrylic paint (liquid, not tube)
- eyedropper
- magnifying glass (or overhead projector)

## Background
Most objects in nature aren't formed of squares or triangles, but of more complicated geometric figures. The term *fractal* describes these figures. A *fractal*—from the Latin fractus, or "broken"—is a complex fragmented geometric shape that can be subdivided into parts, each of which is a reduced-size copy of the whole. Fractals are generally self-similar and independent of scale.

Many natural objects—trees, clouds, mountains, coastlines—are fractals. There are also many mathematical structures that are fractals. What they all have in common is infinite detail. The closer you look at a fractal, the more you see.

Fractals are a part of fractal geometry. Unlike conventional geometry, which is concerned with regular shapes and whole-number dimensions, fractal geometry deals with natural shapes that have noninteger, or fractal, dimensions.

Today, mathematical models of fractal behavior have been applied to such diverse fields as economics, meteorology, and computer graphics.

This project creates a simple fractal design by combining two materials of different viscosities.

## Procedure
A drop of acrylic paint is pressed between the halves of a CD jewel case. The halves are pulled apart and the resulting pattern is observed.

## Hypothesis
The pattern will show randomness, complexity, and self-similarity—the three key attributes of a fractal.

## Experiment to Test Hypothesis
**1.** Carefully pull apart the two halves of the CD jewel case. Place one half of the case on a flat surface with the hollow part facing down.

**2.** Place a single drop of acrylic paint in the center of the case. Hold the other half of the jewel case, hollow part facing up, over the drop.

**3.** Quickly and evenly push the two halves together so that the paint spreads out into a thin circle between them. Pick up the two halves and press them firmly together, using your thumbs.

**4.** Immediately pull the halves straight apart in one motion and observe the resulting pattern of paint. Allow the paint to dry for about 20 minutes.

**5.** Examine the pattern through a magnifying glass or place the jewel case on an overhead projector.

### Results & Conclusions

Pulling the jewel-case halves apart produced a circular blot filled with intricately branched patterns resembling the veins in a leaf. The "veins" were thick in the middle and branched into finer divisions near the edges.

Examining the patterns with a magnifying glass showed that the branches at the edge divided into finer and finer filaments that appeared to continue infinitely in ever-shrinking scales. Placing the pattern on an overhead projector confirmed this. The randomness of the pattern, its lack of scale, and the fact that the whole of the pattern resembled something found in Nature (the veins of a leaf) convinced us that this was a true fractal.

But how did it happen? The answer lies in the different viscosities of acrylic paint and air. The term *viscosity* means how easily something flows. Something like paint (or chocolate syrup, or even ketchup) has a high viscosity because it resists its own flow. Air, on the other hand, has a low viscosity. When high-viscosity paint spread into low-viscosity air, the paint flowed into a circular disk. But when the halves were pulled apart and the air spread into the paint, the air created a fractal pattern.

Looking closely at our fractal showed us that fingers of air had penetrated into the paint. These fingers spawned smaller fingers at random, which spawned even smaller fingers. The resulting "leaf" contained fingers of air at many different scales. So our pattern had the basic qualities of a true fractal: randomness and similarity over many different sizes and scales.

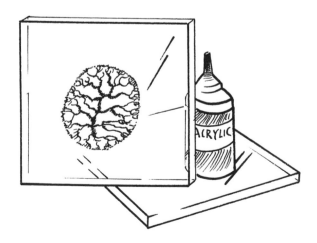

# Geometric Fallacies

*Can we disprove the geometric fallacy that suggests that recombining the parts of one shape into another shape will result in a net gain or loss of area?*

## Materials
- cardstock
- marker
- ruler
- dollar bill from Monopoly board game
- photocopier (machine)
- scissors

**Note:** *We use play money here because it's illegal to photocopy, photograph, or otherwise copy real money.*

## Background
Geometric shapes that, when cut up and recombined, appear to gain or lose area have made for amusing puzzles for hundreds of years. The writer and mathematician Lewis Carroll was very fond of these *geometric fallacies,* and a collection of his favorites was found among his personal items after his death.

The puzzles demonstrate something called *concealed distribution.* This means that something is concealed in the way something is put together. The fallacy exists because, in the recombination of a shape's components, the shape appears to lose or gain area. Mathematicians know this is impossible, and the following project attempts to debunk the fallacy.

## Procedure
An 8-inch (20-cm) square is cut up and reassembled into a rectangle with an apparent gain of 1 square inch (6.45 square cm). Ten one-dollar Monopoly bills are photocopied, then cut up and reassembled so that we wind up with eleven one-dollar bills. Both procedures are examined for signs of concealed distribution.

## Hypothesis
Upon close examination, the reassembled figures will reveal areas of concealed distribution.

## Experiment to Test Hypothesis
**1.** Cut an 8-inch (20-cm) square from the cardstock and use the marker to divide it into four sections, following the diagram. Label the sections with letters. Multiply the length of one edge by the length of another edge to get the total number of square inches contained in the square.

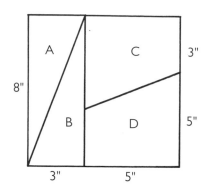

8x8 = 64 square inches (or, roughly
20x20 cm = 400 square cm)

**2.** Cut out the sections and rearrange them into the following rectangle. Multiply the length of a short edge by the length of a long edge to get the total number of square inches.

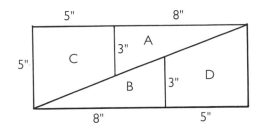

5x13 = 65 square inches (or, roughly
12.5x32.5 = 406 square cm)

Where did the extra square inch come from?

**3.** Make 7 copies of a Monopoly dollar bill (from play money) and cut them out. Arrange the 7 bills in a column. Cut a piece from each bill, following the drawing. But don't separate the pieces, and keep the bills in the same column arrangement you started with.

**4.** Now, move all the cut pieces on the left down the column by one bill, and tape those pieces to the pieces on the right. You will wind up with a new column of 8 bills instead of 7. Notice how the top and bottom bills of the column consist of uncut pieces. Where did the extra dollar come from?

7 bills

8 bills

## Results & Conclusions

A geometric fallacy works because of an almost invisible imperfection in the "larger" piece assembled from the "smaller" piece. In the case of the square that gained a square inch when it was reassembled into a rectangle, a closer look revealed that something wasn't quite right about the rectangle. Even if we'd used the straightest ruler to mark our lines and had the steadiest hand when cutting out the shapes, the two halves of the diagonally divided rectangle would never quite fit together. Looking closely, we could see that the diagonal line was actually a very narrow quadrilateral space with an area of about 1 square inch (6.5 square cm). This meant that the gained square inch was an illusion.

The dollar-bill trick was just another version of the illusion. Since the area removed from each bill was small enough (and the face of a bill so complicated), it was hardly noticeable that a sliver of each bill had been removed and added to another bill. Of course, the more bills used for this trick, the less noticeable the imperfections in each bill. But cutting up 100 bills just to gain a few extra ones seems like an awful lot of work! Unfortunately, turning dollars into more dollars is just a fallacy—at least a geometric one.

Interestingly, fallacies decrease in higher mathematics. Number tricks are common in arithmetic and algebra, and not quite as common in geometry. Trigonometry has only one fallacy, and calculus has none.

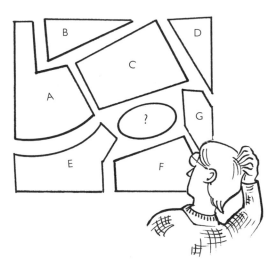

# Hexagonal Close Packing

*Can the hexagonal packing and dislocation lines of atoms be simulated with ball bearings?*

## Materials

- 2-mm (small) ball bearings (or BBs)
- bowl-shaped plate of clear glass
- tweezers

## Background

In nature, hexagons are everywhere. Whether we look into beehives, synthetic substances, living tissue, or even atoms, we can find surprising examples of a characteristic hexagonal pattern. Mathematicians call it *hexagonal close packing*, and it is the most effective way to pack the largest number of same-size objects into a minimum space.

Some obvious examples of hexagonal close packing would be the stack of oranges in the grocery store. Or a group of drinking straws pressed closely together in a jar. Look at the sheet of bubbles that forms in a bathtub. If the bubbles are all about the same size, they arrange themselves in hexagons.

Hexagonal close packing consists of a planar arrangement of units where the alternating rows are staggered. Each unit of the packing makes a parallelogram, and the combined parallelograms create a pattern of six points around a central point, or hexagon. This is a very efficient way to fill space. In a square-packing arrangement of aligned rows, only 52% of a given volume is filled. A hexagonal packing of staggered rows fills 74% of the same volume.

With a magnifying glass or microscope, you can see even smaller examples of hexagonal close packing. Look at the polystyrene beads that make up a Styrofoam cup. When the raw beads are heated, they expand to fill a mold in the most efficient way possible. And even blood can be hexagonal. When it coagulates around a wound, the platelets pack into a hexagonal lattice.

Hexagonal packing makes a lot of sense for atoms. Solid matter is built up from the packing together of atoms, which have the shape of spheres. The empty spaces between spherical atoms are fewer and smaller in a hexagonal arrangement because each atom nestles in the depression between the two atoms below it. But, as this project will demonstrate, hexagonal close packing can be altered in ways that affect both the strength and stability of certain materials—particularly metals and crystals.

## Procedure

A plate is filled with 2-mm ball bearings, one layer thick. The layer is disrupted at the center by removing ball bearings so that various dislocations in the lattice can be observed.

## Hypothesis

The layer of ball bearings will naturally form into a hexagonal close packing arrangement. Each disruption will create new arrangements within the hexagonal lattice, simulating the atomic changes that can occur in metals and crystals.

## Experiment to Test Hypothesis

**1.** Find a wide, shallow plate of smooth glass. If the plate is transparent, you can place it on an overhead projector for a great demonstration.

**2.** Spill about 1 cup (240 ml) of ball bearings into the plate and smooth them out until you have one layer. Allow the layer to crawl partially up the sides of the plate.

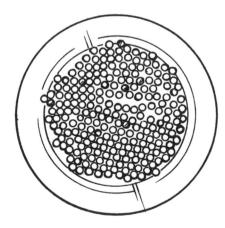

Hexagonal close packing showing point defects and linear dislocations.

**3.** Gently tap the side of the plate with your finger and notice any shift in the ball bearings.

**4.** Use the tweezers to remove clusters of balls from the center of the plate. Tap the plate and watch what happens.

## Results & Conclusions

After pouring and smoothing them into a single layer, the ball bearings immediately arranged themselves into the staggered rows of a hexagonal close-packing pattern. But the pattern wasn't uniform and showed gaps, dislocation lines, and areas where the balls seemed jumbled together. The edges of the layer were also chaotic and jagged. Removing clusters of balls with the tweezers from the center of the plate made this situation even worse.

Tapping the plate began to change this. With each tap, the open spaces at the center of the plate began to close up. But, as our hypothesis predicted, these were replaced by new open spaces radiating outward. It appeared that, with each tap, larger areas of ball bearings were becoming more uniform toward the center, with dislocations and gaps moving out toward the edges.

One of the most noticeable disruptions was a *point defect*, where one ball was missing. Tapping the plate didn't make the empty point disappear, because a ball moving into it left another open space behind. It seemed that point defects could only disappear by working their way out to the edge of the layer. Another type of disruption, *linear dislocation*, appeared when one row of balls didn't exactly fit into the empty spaces of a neighboring row.

The result was a kind of fracture line where the balls on either side of the line were packed into squares instead of hexagons. The squares took up more space, and like the point defects, could be fixed only by moving out to the edges of the plate with more tapping.

After about 2 minutes of tapping, most of the ball bearings were in a near-perfect hexagonal close-packing pattern. Even the edges had begun to form into neat rows with only a few imperfections. Presumably, if the tapping were regular enough and had continued for hours, the ball bearings would have formed a perfect hexagon
in the plate.

Tapping the plate moved imperfections out of the ball bearings just as heating a metal hardens the metal. This is also true for heating crystals. When we heat a metal or crystal we *anneal* it. Annealing makes a material stronger but less flexible. Metals made up of large crystals are strong but brittle. Metals with smaller crystals are pliable, but not quite as strong.

To show this, we took a thick brass wire and began bending it back and forth. The wire, very flexible at first, began to grow stiff by the fifth or sixth bend—as if actually growing stronger. A few more bends and it snapped. Bending the wire allowed the imperfections in the hexagonal close-packing pattern to work themselves out. The arrangement of atoms, although tighter, was now less flexible and subject to breakage. This proves that it's sometimes better to allow for a little imperfection!

# Möbius Loop Mysteries

*Will cutting apart a Möbius loop and its variations produce completely different shapes?*

## Materials
- two 11x14-inch (27.94x35.56-cm) sheets of paper
- ruler
- marker
- scissors
- glue

## Background
*Topology* is the branch of mathematics that studies how shapes can change into different shapes while keeping some of their original qualities. Unlike geometry, topology views a circle and a square as two different forms of the same object. Topologists call the changing qualities of a shape *variants* and the unchanging qualities *invariants*. One of the best ways to become acquainted with this unusual concept is by playing with a novel object called a Möbius loop,

named after the 19th century German mathematician who discovered it.

A Möbius loop differs from an ordinary loop in several interesting ways. To make an ordinary loop, you connect the ends of a strip of paper so that the resulting loop has two sides, two edges, and an inside and outside. If you draw a line around the inside of the loop, the line joins with itself and remains on the inside. A line drawn on the inside of the loop never meets a line drawn on the outside of the loop and vice versa.

But a Möbius loop is made by taking a strip of paper and giving one end a half-twist before joining it to the other end. This way, the top of the strip also becomes the bottom, and the bottom of the strip also becomes the top. The resulting loop has only one side and one edge. You can prove this by drawing a line around the loop. Eventually, your line goes completely around and meets itself.

There are many variations of Möbius loops that this project will construct with the ultimate aim of cutting them apart to see what other types of shapes they will become. In doing this, the loops will demonstrate some of the basic concepts of topological mathematics.

## Procedure

Six pairs of loops of increasing complexity are constructed. One loop of each pair is cut apart, and the resulting shape is examined against its original for variants and invariants.

## Hypothesis

When cut apart, each loop will transform into a shape that bears little resemblance to the original loop.

## Experiment to Test Hypothesis

1. Cut twelve 1½x14-inch (3.81x35.56 cm) strips of paper from the two sheets. Using the ruler and marker, draw a line up the center of each strip.

2. Glue the ends of the first and second strips together, making two ordinary loops. Cut one of the loops along the line. Compare the whole loop to the cut loop.

3. To make a half-twist Möbius loop, take the next strip and give one end a half twist (180°) before gluing it to the other end. Make one more of these and cut it along the line. Compare the whole loop to the cut one.

4. To make a full-twist Möbius loop, take the next strip and give one end a full twist (360°) before gluing it to the other end. Make one more of these and cut it along the line. Compare the whole loop to the cut one.

5. To make a one-and-a-half-twist Möbius loop, take the next strip and give one end one and a half twists before gluing it to the other end. Make one more of these and cut it along the line. Compare the whole loop to the cut one.

6. To make a perpendicular loop, make two ordinary loops, then glue one loop to the side of the other loop at a right angle. Make one more of these and cut it along the lines, keeping in mind that you will actually make two cuts, one of which will cross the other at a right angle. Compare the whole perpendicular loop to the cut one.

7. On the remaining segment of 11x14-inch (27.94x35.56-cm) paper, glue your sets of loops next to each other. Make a table like the one below to record the number of variants and invariants between the whole and cut loops.

## Type of Loop

| Features | Whole Loop | Cut Loop |
|---|---|---|
| Loops | | |
| Twists | | |
| Sides | | |
| Edges | | |
| Dimensions | | |
| Intertwines | | |

## Results & Conclusions

True to our hypothesis, each cut loop produced surprises. This was true for all loops except the ordinary loop.

We used the remaining piece of paper to display our whole loops beside their cut versions, comparing variants and invariants as shown opposite.

Whole          Cut

Whole          Cut

## Ordinary Loop

| Features | Whole Loop | Cut Loop |
|---|---|---|
| Loops | 1 | 2 |
| Twists | 0 | 0 |
| Sides | 2 | 2 |
| Edges | 2 | 2 |
| Dimensions | 14" circ. | 14" circ. |
| Intertwines | 0 | 0 |

Invariants = 5 / Variants = 1

## Full-Twist Möbius Loop

| Features | Whole Loop | Cut Loop |
|---|---|---|
| Loops | 1 | 2 |
| Twists | 1 | 1 |
| Sides | 2 | 2 |
| Edges | 2 | 2 |
| Dimensions | 14" circ. | 28" circ. |
| Intertwines | 0 | 1 |

Invariants = 3 / Variants = 3

Whole          Cut

Whole          Cut

## Half-Twist Möbius Loop

| Features | Whole Loop | Cut Loop |
|---|---|---|
| Loops | 1 | 1 |
| Twists | 0.5 | 2 |
| Sides | 1 | 2 |
| Edges | 1 | 2 |
| Dimensions | 14" circ. | 28" circ. |
| Intertwines | 0 | 0 |

Invariants = 2 / Variants = 4

## One-and-a-Half-Twist Möbius Loop

| Features | Whole Loop | Cut Loop |
|---|---|---|
| Loops | 1 | 1 |
| Twists | 1.5 | 3 |
| Sides | 1 | 1 |
| Edges | 1 | 1 |
| Dimensions | 14"circ. | 28" circ. |
| Intertwines | 0 | 3 |

Invariants = 3 / Variants = 3

Whole                          Cut

## Perpendicular Loop

| Features | Whole Loop | Cut Loop |
|---|---|---|
| Loops | 2 | 1 |
| Twists | 0 | 0 |
| Sides | 4 | 2 |
| Edges | 4 | 2 |
| Dimensions | 28" circ. | 14" square |
| Intertwines | 0 | 0 |

Invariants = 2 / Variants = 4

Both the one-and-a-half-twist Möbius loop and the perpendicular loop showed special transformations. For the one-and-a-half-twist loop, the number of twists doubled upon cutting the loop, but the cut loop produced a knot that was impossible to untangle by twisting alone. The whole perpendicular loop became a perfect square after cutting, with sides half the dimension of the combined circumferences of the perpendicular loops.

Of the five loop examples, two loops (the half-twist and the perpendicular) showed more variants than invariants when cut. This meant that they became objects substantially transformed by the cutting. Two other loops (one-and-a-half-twist and full-twist) showed an equal number of invariants and variants. These loops were as much the same as different after cutting. As expected, the ordinary loop was more the same than different after cutting. All of the loops demonstrated interesting concepts in topology.

# Number Combinations in Dice

*In a series of 100 dice rolls, will some scores occur more frequently than others?*

## Materials
- 2 dice
- 20 checkers
- oaktag
- marker
- calculator
- pencil
- paper

## Background
The use of dice is popular in wagering, board games, and even some card games. Each of the six sides of a single die is marked with one to six dots, so that two dice thrown together yield 36 possible scores, from 2 to 12. Some games, like Craps, are designed around the odds that certain dice scores will occur much more frequently than others. This project tests that assumption.

## Procedure
After calculating all possible dice combinations for scores 2 through 12, a pair of dice is thrown 100 times. Two players claim or relinquish checkers depending upon whether a "winning" or "losing" score is rolled. A running tally of each score is kept and, after 100 rolls, the totals are entered numerically into a table. The table is examined for evidence that some scores occur more frequently than others.

## Hypothesis
Although certain scores will seem to appear more frequently, the odds are evenly distributed among all possible scores.

## Experiment to Test Hypothesis
**1.** Draw a table like the one below. Make sure the first column has three sections divided into two shades. Or use two different colors if you like.

| 2 Dice Score | # Combinations Possible for Score | Approximate Percentage | How Many Times Per 100 Rolls |
|---|---|---|---|
| 2 | x | x | x |
| 3 | x | x | x |
| 4 | x | x | x |
| 5 | x | x | x |
| 6 | x | x | x |
| 7 | x | x | x |
| 8 | x | x | x |
| 9 | x | x | x |
| 10 | x | x | x |
| 11 | x | x | x |
| 12 | x | x | x |

**2.** By placing the dice in front of you and turning them when necessary, figure out how many combinations of dice can produce each score. Enter these data into the second column.

**3.** To calculate percentages, divide 36 by each score and then divide 100 by the quotient. You now have "hard" data for each score—the number of combinations possible for each and what percent each claims in a total of 100 rolls.

**4.** Divide the checkers between you and your partner. Let your partner roll the dice while you keep a running total on a piece of paper. If your partner's score is any of those contained in the dark gray boxes, he or she loses and gives you a checker. If your partner's score is any of those contained in the lighter gray boxes, he or she wins and claims a checker.

**5.** Continue to the hundredth roll—even if you or your partner have run out of checkers. If you both have checkers left at the hundredth roll, compare your totals.

**6.** Add up the tallies for each score and enter them numerically in the table. Examine all data on the table for patterns and inconsistencies.

## Results & Conclusions

Calculations alone proved our hypothesis incorrect. Although at first it appeared that all scores of a dice have an equal chance of turning up, the data revealed that some scores are six times more likely to turn up than other scores. This mathematical bias occurred because some scores could be created with several combinations of numbers.

The bias was clearly demonstrated in the checker game that followed. Although "luck" seemed to be with the roller for the first 20 rolls, the tide steadily turned, so that the eighty-ninth roll—yet another loser—removed the last checker from the roller.

Our completed table looked like this.

| 2 Dice Score | # Combinations Possible for Score | Approximate Percentage | How Many Times Per 100 Rolls |
|---|---|---|---|
| 2 | 1 | 2.8% | 3 |
| 3 | 2 | 5.6% | 5 |
| 4 | 3 | 8.3% | 9 |
| 5 | 4 | 11.1% | 11 |
| 6 | 5 | 13.8% | 14 |
| 7 | 6 | 16.6% | 17 |
| 8 | 5 | 13.8% | 15 |
| 9 | 4 | 11.1% | 10 |
| 10 | 3 | 8.3% | 8 |
| 11 | 2 | 5.6% | 4 |
| 12 | 1 | 2.8% | 4 |

Many wagering games, such as Craps, are configured so those scores of 2 through 4 and 9 through 12 are winning rolls. Since a total of 10 scores out of a possible 12 appear to win, the odds of winning at dice seem better than 50%. But the trap is in the combinations. Although only 4 of the 12 scores (5–8) appear to lose, the odds can be *up to six times as great* that the two dice will produce them. Board games are similarly scaled on the assumption that the most likely rolls of the dice will be 5–8.

# Plot a Cardioid

Adult Help Required

*Will one circle, rolled completely around the perimeter of a second circle, result in two complete rotations of the rolled circle, tracing a cardioid?*

## Materials

- two sets of 6-inch (15.24-cm or 15-cm) diameter plywood disks
- two sets of 4-inch (10.16-cm or 10-cm) diameter plywood disks
- 2 wooden spools
- white posterboard
- white paper
- Sharpie pen
- ¾-inch (18-mm) hex nut
- 1x⅜-inch (25.4x9.5-mm, or 25x10-mm) spacer
- metal coat hanger
- spray adhesive (medium tack)
- white glue
- tape measure
- scissors
- drill
- ¾-inch (18-mm) drill bit
- wire cutter
- adult helper

**Caution:** *An electric drill is a serious power tool and should be handled only by an adult.*

## Background

The word *cardioid* comes from the Greek root *cardi*, meaning heart. The graceful heart-shaped curve of a cardioid fascinates mathematicians because it shows an interesting relationship between two circles of the same size. For example, think of two circles as wheels with the same radii. If one wheel rolls completely around the edge of the other wheel, the rolling wheel makes two complete rotations before returning to its starting point. If you attached a pencil to the edge of the rolling wheel, it would trace out a cardioid shape around the fixed wheel.

Cardioids are useful because they can show the interference and congruence patterns of waves that radiate concentrically from a point source. In doing so, they can identify the areas of greatest sensitivity on microphones or antennas. By calculating a polar plot on such devices, engineers can determine how best to design or position the device so sound waves or electromagnetic radiation doesn't distort. For example, a cardioid

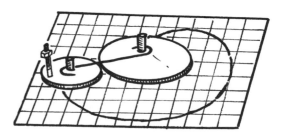

microphone is sensitive to front sound and minimizes rear sound. The "null" spot of the microphone occurs at 180°, where the cardioid curve meets itself. In the same way, a directional cardioid antenna minimizes the static signals from peripheral radiation and delivers a clearer sound or image to a receiver.

Although the mathematics can get complicated, plotting the cardioid and its variations has rewarded physicists, mathematicians, and engineers with a valuable understanding of wave relationships. The aim of this project is much more modest. With the help of two plywood disks and charcoal, the unique relationship between circles of a cardioid will be demonstrated graphically.

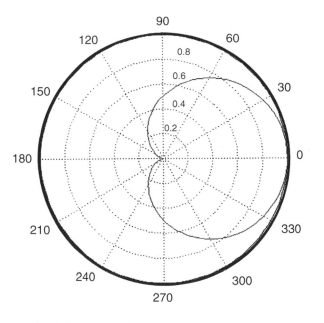

Polar plot of the sensitivity pattern on a cardioid microphone.

## Procedure

Two disks of the same size are joined so that one is fixed and the other can move around it. A weighted Sharpie pen is attached to the moving disk to trace out the resulting shape on posterboard.

## Hypothesis

The combined motions of rotation and revolution in the moving disk will produce a cardioid.

## Experiment to Test Hypothesis

**1.** Place a 6-inch (15-cm) disk on the paper and trace around it with the pencil. Remove the disk.

**2.** Use the ruler to draw a vertical line along each side of the traced circle and a horizontal line at the top and bottom. Make the lines long enough to intersect, forming a square.

**3.** Connect opposite corners of the square with lines. The intersection of diagonal lines indicates the center of the circle.

**4.** Cut the circle from the paper to create a template for drilling holes. Apply a little spray adhesive to the blank side. Glue the template to the disk.

**5.** When the glue dries, drill a hole through the center of the disk, guided by the template. Carefully peel off the paper (you'll use it again). Drill a second hole in the disk as close to the edge as possible. Make the hole wide enough to contain the spacer, which you should push down so that the bottom of the spacer is flush with the lower surface of the disk.

**6.** Attach the template to the second 6-inch (15-cm) disk and drill a hole through the center. Then take one of the 4-inch (10-cm) disks to make another template, which you'll use to drill center holes.

**7.** The holes are used as guides only. Line up the center holes of the smaller and larger disks and glue the small disks to the large ones. Turn the disks over and glue the spools over the center holes. Allow the glue to dry overnight.

**8.** Cut an 11-inch (about 28 cm) length of wire from the hanger. Measure 1¾ inches (about 4.5 cm) from each end and, using your fingers, carefully bend each end around a spool. The hooks at each end of the wire should face in opposite directions and connect the disks.

**9.** Spray the bottom of the 6-inch (15-cm) disk (single hole) with adhesive and attach it to the center of clean white oaktag. Place the two-hole disk above it.

**10.** Rotate the two-hole disk until the hole at the edge is against the edge of the single-hole disk. The hole should be just to the left of the hanger. Remove the cap of the Sharpie pen and insert it in the hole at the edge. Put the hex nut over the pen shaft to weigh it down.

**11.** Grasp the spool of the two-hole disk firmly. In a slow, steady, uninterrupted motion, twist the spool to the right so that the disk turns. The pen should leave a trace line behind it. When the pen reaches its starting position, the cardioid is complete.

### Results & Conclusions

Guided by the disk, the sweep of the pen around the poster board produced a beautiful cardioid. The curve streamed behind as the disk completed its first 360° rotation (at the halfway point of the cardioid). But the curve was hidden by the disk as it completed its second rotation, closing the cardioid.

The joined disk design works for experimenting with other curve combinations. We found that disks of smaller sizes could be attached to the center disk and moved to trace new designs, each of which revealed surprises.

# The Chaos Game

*Will random throws of a colored die produce a regular fractal pattern?*

## Materials
- 1 die (not reusable)
- red, blue, and green permanent markers
- white cardstock
- small coin
- ruler

## Background
A fractal—from the Latin *fractus*, or "broken"—is a complex fragmented geometric shape that can be subdivided in parts, each of which is a reduced-size copy of the whole. Fractals are unique in geometry because a fractal has a finite area but infinite perimeters. The more closely you look at a fractal, the more detail you see, and this detail takes the form of self-similarity. Such unusual qualities make fractals fascinating objects to mathematicians.

Many natural objects—trees, clouds, mountains, and coastlines—are shaped like fractals. And dynamic systems, such as the movement of oceans or storms, can be represented mathematically by fractals. Fractals provide a new mathematical language in which to describe complex and apparently chaotic events in nature.

This project demonstrates how the apparently random throws of dice can be represented in fractal geometry.

## Procedure
Opposite sides of a die are painted in three colors: red, blue, and green. The vertices of a triangle are marked with the same colors. The die is rolled 100 times and the rolls are plotted between the vertices.

## Hypothesis
The apparent randomness of the rolled die will result in a fractal pattern.

## Experiment to Test Hypothesis
**1.** At the top edge and two bottom corners of the cardstock, draw three dots—red, green, and blue—indicating the vertices of a triangle. Don't draw the triangle.

**2.** Color the opposite sides of the die red, green, and blue.

**3.** Choose any spot inside the triangle as your starting point. Place the coin there.

**4.** Roll the die. Depending on what color comes up, move the coin half the distance to the appropriately colored vertex. That is, if red comes up, move the coin half the distance to the red vertex, using the ruler if necessary.

**5.** From this position, roll the die again and move the coin to a new position half the distance to the colored vertex. Continue this procedure for another eight rolls for a total of ten rolls.

**6.** For the eleventh roll, remove the coin, and mark the new position indicated by the roll of the die with one of the colored markers. For example, if the die rolls green, make a green dot at the halfway point between your current position and the green vertex. If the die rolls blue, make a blue dot halfway to the blue vertex.

**7.** Continue rolling and marking dots for about a hundred rolls. Observe the results.

### Results & Conclusions

After about thirty throws of the die a clear pattern could be seen emerging in the three colors: a pattern of nested triangles. The greater the number of throws, the more detail emerged from the triangles until a pattern resembling the one at right eventually emerged.

This was a classic fractal pattern called the Sierpinski triangle, named after the Polish mathematician who discovered it in 1915. After a hundred throws, it was clear that the pattern would self-replicate infinitely.

In the Chaos Game, the first throw of the die is called the *seed*. The process of repeating the throws and tracing the resulting movement is called the *orbit of the seed*. The orbit is guided into creating the triangle by what mathematicians call a *strange attractor*. The result was a graphic representation, in fractal geometry, of an apparently chaotic process.

The amazing thing about the Sierpinski triangle is that the triangle results no matter where the seed is started. Our seed began equidistant from the three vertices. By the second throw (red), it hopped half the distance to one of the three next-smaller triangles. These smaller triangles represented all points half the distance from the vertices of the largest triangle. After one more iteration, the point moved into an even smaller triangle, which represented all points half the distance from the previous triangle, and so on into infinity. These reductions can't be represented by whole numbers and are described as "fractal fractions."

Sierpinski Triangle

# Visualize Prime Numbers

*Is it possible to visualize prime numbers geometrically?*

## Materials
- box of wooden play cubes
- 2 large posterboards
- cellophane tape
- marker
- flat surface

## Background
A prime number is defined by mathematicians as any number greater than 1 that can be divided evenly only by itself and the number 1. Prime numbers—especially very large ones—are not only mathematical curiosities but are generated by computers to create useful encryption algorithms. Whenever someone sends a credit-card number over the Internet, the number gets encrypted by the browser. This encryption algorithm is based on the theory of prime numbers.

This project will determine, out of a list of 20 numbers, which numbers can be turned into squares and rectangles and which numbers won't cooperate. In doing this, we will visualize some of the unique properties of prime numbers.

## Procedure
Cubes are arranged to reflect each number—prime and composite—in a list of 20 numbers.

## Hypothesis
Prime numbers will be unable to generate squares or rectangles other than in a single row.

## Experiment to Test Hypothesis
**1.** Tape the two posterboards together horizontally. Make two columns of numbers on the joined boards, the first at the left edge and the second at the seam. List the numbers 1 to 10 in the first column and 11 to 20 in the second column.

**2.** Place a single cube next to number 1. Place two cubes next to number 2. Place three cubes next to number 3, and so on, until you have a quantity of cubes corresponding to each number in the list.

**3.** Go down the list and try to assemble each quantity of cubes into as many squares or rectangles as you can. Which numbers just won't work?

# Cube Patterns for 20 Numbers

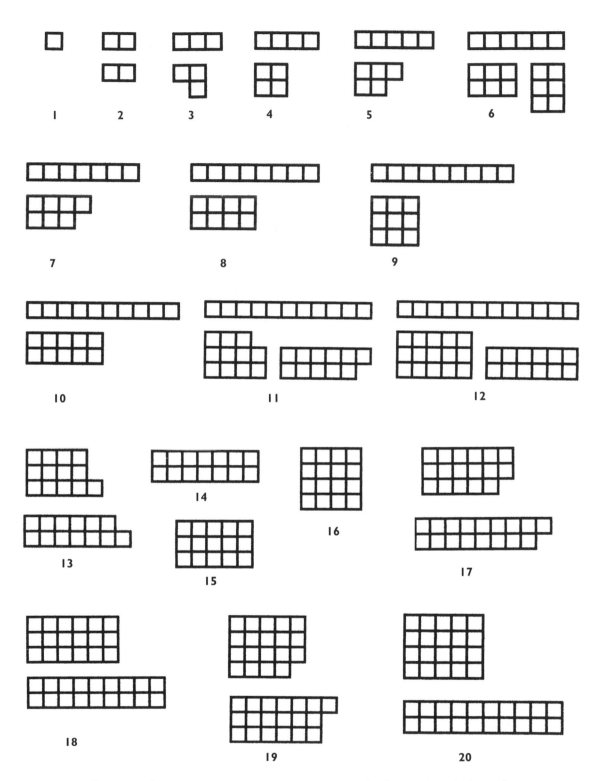

Prime numbers cannot generate squares or rectangles (except in a single row).

## Results & Conclusions

Our hypothesis was correct in stating that prime numbers were unable to generate squares or rectangles other than in a row. The results of our cube patterns for each of the 20 numbers are shown on page 217.

Although it might not seem so at first, knowing the spatial equivalent of a prime number might prove useful someday. For example, it could help you determine whether that quantity of odd-lot tiles that's been in the garage for the past several years would be sufficient for covering the floor of your rectangular laundry room!

# Index

post-sunset green flash and, 150–152
refraction angles of, 173–174
retinal afterimage and, 52–53, 150–151
scattering of, 181–182
of sky, stimulating, 181–182
starlight refraction patterns, 157–159
wavelengths, 181
light years, defined, 157
linear dislocations, 203–204
liquefaction, 175
liquid; *see also* soft drinks; water
colloidal suspension, 178
dehydrating juice, 126–127
densities of, 101–102, 122–123
homogenized, 132
immiscible, 134
measurements, 10, 5
Newtonian fluids, 177
non-Newtonian fluid properties, 177–178
polymer crystals in, 126–127
viscosity of, 177, 178, 198
loads, on bridges, 112
lumber measurements, 10
lung capacity
aging and, 34–36
measuring, 34, 35
of men, 34
normal, 34
sample test results, 36
of women, 34

**M**
magnetic garnet, 156
magnetism
affecting atomic particles, 107
balancing gravity and, 109
diamagnetism, 70, 75–76, 77–78, 105, 107–109
ferromagnetism, 70, 75, 77
levitating magnet with, 107–109
negative magnetic susceptibility, 75, 77
paramagnetism, 70, 71, 75, 77
magnetite
detecting, 68–69
in sand, 156
magnet-related projects
Aluminum Air Battery, 62–63

Cellular Phone EMR & Topography, 64–65
Cellular Phone EMR & Weather, 66–67
Detecting Magnetite, 68–69
Fast & Slow Magnets, 70–71
Miniscule Motor, 72–74
Repulsive Prunes, 75–76
Strange Levitating Magnet, 107–109
Strange Water, 77–78
magnets; *see also* electromagnetism; magnetism
attraction classifications of, 70, 75, 77
as electrical "air-bags," 71
fast and slow, 70–71
induction and, 70
levitating, 107–109
neodymium, 70, 72, 73, 75–76, 77, 78, 107–109
from outer space, 156
poles of, 72, 74, 107
Make a Polymer Jelly, 128–129
Mars
Earth compared to, 153–154
order of planets and, 153
size of, 153–154
mass, simulating attraction of, 148–149
materials, 8, 10
math projects
Calculate Bicycle Gear Ratios, 188–191
The Chaos Game, 214–215
A Different Shape for Dice, 184–187
Fibonacci Model of Plant Growth, 192–196
Fractals in Acrylic, 197–198
Geometric Fallacies, 199–201
Hexagonal Close Packing, 202–204
Mobius Loop Mysteries, 205–208
Number Combinations in Dice, 209–210
Plot a Cardioid, 211–213
Visualize Prime Numbers, 216–218
measurements, 10, 5
Astronomical Units (AUs), 140, 141
Dry-Matter Basis (DMB), 24
of heavenly bodies, 141
metric, 5, 10

"pinch," 45
Measure Sugar in Soft Drinks, 130–131
Measure the Protein in Commercial Cat Foods, 24–26
memory
chewing gum and, 39–40
hippocampus and, 39
insulin and, 39
muscle activity and, 39
smelling rosemary and, 54–55
Mercury, 153
metals, hexagonal close packing of, 202–204
Meteoric Sand, 155–156
meteors
craters from, 145–147
major showers of, 155
micrometeors in sand, 155–156
meter, defined, 5, 103, 147, 5
metric equivalents, 5
micrometeors, 155–156
micrometer
homemade, 116–118
inventor of, 116
uses of, 116
milk
Coriolis effect in, 134
emulsifiers in, 132, 134
homogenized, 132
separating components in, 132–133
swirls in, 134
millimeter, defined, 5
Miniscule Motor, 72–74
mobile phones; *see* cell phone(s)
Mobius loop
illustrating topological concepts, 205–208
making, 205
mysteries, 205–208
ordinary loop vs., 205
variants/invariants of, 205, 206, 207–208
variations of, 206–208
molds
characteristics of, 88
honey controlling, 88–89
types of, 89
molecules
altering structure of, 128–129
capillary action of, 115, 120
identifying sizes of, 120–121
spectral emission of, 142
water, 104
mongrel dogs, 14
motors
armatures in, 72, 74

electromagnetism and, 72–74
enabling automation, 72
mechanics of, 72
Miniscule Motor, 72–74
rotary, 72–74
uses of, 72
muscle activity, memory and, 39
music
affecting dinner, 41–43
conversation and, 41–43, 49
different pitches, 17–18
dogs hearing, 17–18
exercise duration and, 49–51
frequency ranges, 17
Mozart vs. popular, 43

**N**
nature
Fibonacci plant model, 192–196
fractal patterns in, 197, 198, 214
negative magnetic susceptibility, 75, 77
neodymium magnets, 70, 72, 73, 75–76, 77, 78, 107–109
Neptune, 153
nerve(s); *see also* neuropathic pain
cell, illustrated, 60
speed of sensations, 59
neuropathic pain
defined, 59
simulating, 59–60
spatial summation, 60
thermal-grill illusion and, 59–60
Newtonian and non-Newtonian fluids, 177–178
nitrogen, in air, 135
noncrystalline particles, 178
Non-Newtonian Two-Step, 177–178
Number Combinations in Dice, 209–210
number recall, rosemary and, 54–55

**O**
obligate carnivores, 24
octahedron, 184, 185, 186
Odyssey of the Mind, 10, 11
oil (crude) extraction, 175
orange juice, dehydrating, 126–127
organization of projects, in this book, 8–9
oxidation (rust), 135–136